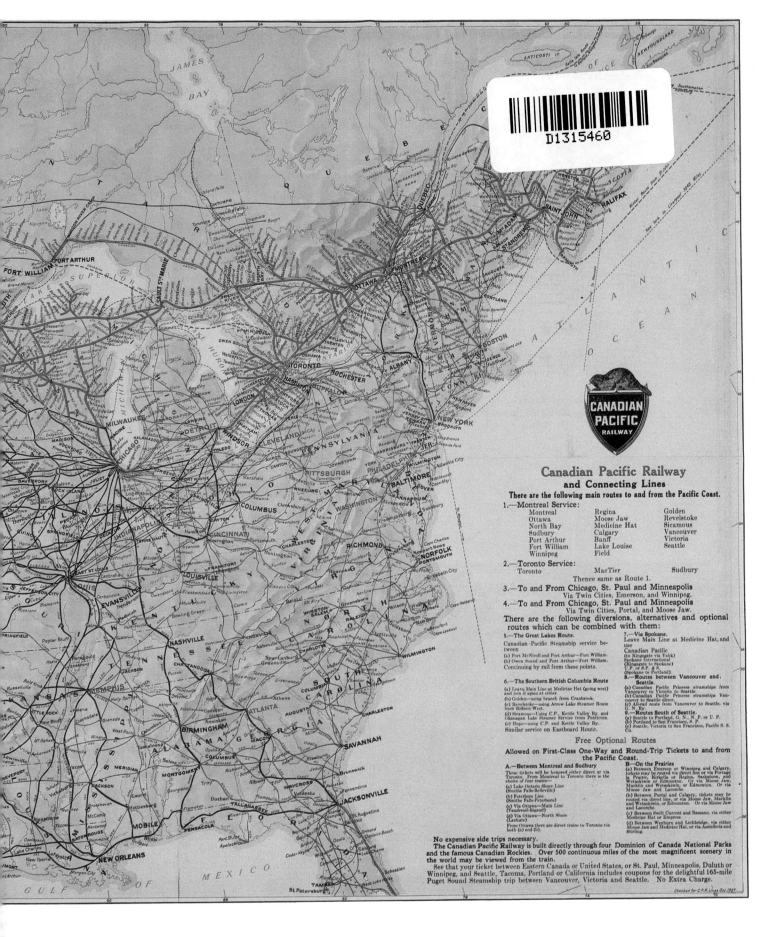

Canadian Pacific Railway
and Connecting Lines

There are the following main routes to and from the Pacific Coast.

1.—Montreal Service:

Montreal	Regina	Golden
Ottawa	Moose Jaw	Revelstoke
North Bay	Medicine Hat	Sicamous
Sudbury	Calgary	Vancouver
Port Arthur	Banff	Victoria
Fort William	Lake Louise	Seattle
Winnipeg	Field	

2.—Toronto Service:

Toronto   MacTier   Sudbury

Thence same as Route 1.

3.—To and From Chicago, St. Paul and Minneapolis
Via Twin Cities, Emerson, and Winnipeg.

4.—To and From Chicago, St. Paul and Minneapolis
Via Twin Cities, Portal, and Moose Jaw.

There are the following diversions, alternatives and optional routes which can be combined with them:

5.—The Great Lakes Route.
Canadian Pacific Steamship service between

(a) Port McNicoll and Port Arthur—Fort William.
(b) Owen Sound and Port Arthur—Fort William.
Continuing by rail from these points.

6.—The Southern British Columbia Route

(a) Leave Main Line at Medicine Hat (going west) and join it again at either
(b) Golden—using branch from Cranbrook.
(c) Revelstoke—using Arrow Lake Steamer Route from Robson West.
(d) Sicamous—Using C.P., Kettle Valley Ry. and Okanagan Lake Steamer Service from Penticton.
(e) Hope—using C.P. and Kettle Valley Ry.
Similar service on Eastbound Route.

7.—Via Spokane.
Leave Main Line at Medicine Hat, and use

Canadian Pacific
(to Kingsgate via Yahk)
Spokane International
(Kingsgate to Spokane)
U.P. of S.P. R.R.
(Spokane to Portland).

8.—Routes between Vancouver and Seattle.

(a) Canadian Pacific Princess steamship from Vancouver to Victoria to Seattle.
(b) Canadian Pacific Princess steamship Vancouver to Seattle direct.
(c) All-rail route from Vancouver to Seattle, via G. N. Ry.

9.—Routes South of Seattle.

(a) Seattle to Portland, G. N., N.P. or U.P.
(b) Portland to San Francisco, S. P.
(c) Seattle, Victoria to San Francisco, Pacific S. S. Co.

Free Optional Routes

Allowed on First-Class One-Way and Round-Trip Tickets to and from the Pacific Coast.

A.—Between Montreal and Sudbury
These tickets will be honored either direct or via Toronto. From Montreal to Toronto there is the choice of four routes—
(a) Lake Ontario Shore Line (Smiths Falls-Belleville)
(b) Peterboro Line (Smiths Falls-Peterboro)
(c) Via Ottawa—Main Line (Vaudreuil-Rigaud)
(d) Via Ottawa—North Shore (Lachute)
From Ottawa there are direct trains to Toronto via both (a) and (b).

B.—On the Prairies
(a) Between Emerson or Winnipeg and Calgary, tickets may be routed via direct line or via Portage la Prairie, Kirkella or Regina, Saskatoon, and Wetaskiwin or Edmonton. Or via Moose Jaw, Macklin and Wetaskiwin, or Edmonton. Or via Moose Jaw and Lacombe.
(b) Between Portal and Calgary, tickets may be routed via direct line, or via Moose Jaw, Macklin and Wetaskiwin, or Edmonton. Or via Moose Jaw and Lacombe.
(c) Between Swift Current and Bassano, via either Medicine Hat or Empress.
(d) Between Weyburn and Lethbridge, via either Moose Jaw and Medicine Hat, or via Assiniboia and Stirling.

No expensive side trips necessary.

The Canadian Pacific Railway is built directly through four Dominion of Canada National Parks and the famous Canadian Rockies. Over 500 continuous miles of the most magnificent scenery in the world may be viewed from the train.

See that your ticket between Eastern Canada or United States, or St. Paul, Minneapolis, Duluth or Winnipeg, and Seattle, Tacoma, Portland or California includes coupons for the delightful 165-mile Puget Sound Steamship trip between Vancouver, Victoria and Seattle. No Extra Charge.

Checked for C.P.R. Lines Oct. 1927

600/mug

TRAIL OF IRON

THE CPR AND
THE BIRTH OF THE WEST, 1880-1930

BILL McKEE and GEORGEEN KLASSEN

Climbing the Rockies.

THE GLENBOW-ALBERTA INSTITUTE
in association with
DOUGLAS & McINTYRE
VANCOUVER/TORONTO

Douglas & McIntyre Ltd.
1615 Venables
Vancouver, British Columbia
V5L 2H1

CANADIAN CATALOGUING IN PUBLICATION DATA

McKee, William Carey, 1946-
   Trail of Iron

Includes index.
Bibliography. p.
ISBN 0-88894-399-7
ISBN 0-88894-413-6 (ltd. ed.)

1. Canadian Pacific Railway
   - History
2. Canada - History I. Title.
HE2810.C2M35   385'.0971   C83-091282-7

Book design: Nancy Grout
and Barbara Hodgson
Typesetting: Vancouver
Typesetting Co. Ltd.
Printed and bound in Canada:
D.W. Friesen & Sons Ltd.

Contents

Nations have many anniversaries and centennials, remembrances of historic moments in time past. Draped in bunting, heralded by parades and unveiled to the drone of eulogies, the monuments to achievement are raised with enthusiasm and then too often abandoned to the frailty of memory and the lingering attention of pigeons.

But in Canadian history there is one great historic fact that cannot be tied to a particular date or year except arbitrarily. It is the political and economic reality of the railway as the narrow thread of steel that bound the nation together. It is that reality which we celebrate in this book and in "The Great CPR Exposition" at the Glenbow Museum. The exhibition is to be opened and the book published on an arbitrary though not illogical date, 11 August 1983, one hundred years to the day after the CPR steel reached the banks of the Bow river and what is now the City of Calgary.

This book, like the exhibition and the national conference of historians being held in September 1983, focusses its attention on the Canadian Pacific transcontinental railway and its pervasive impact on the opening up of the Canadian West. The reader is asked to envisage it in the broader context of the emerging nation.

Britain, faced with the unsettled state of her colonies in Canada, sent out Lord Durham to investigate conditions in 1838. In his report of 1839, he saw not only the need for responsible government but recognized the importance of linking the colonies together with bonds of commerce and communication. The idea of an intercolonial railway, drawing together the Maritimes, Lower and Upper Canada, was thus conceived, and its promise played no small part in the Confederation of those colonies in 1867, even though the railway system was not completed until 1876.

Two years after Confederation, the Central and Union Pacific railroad had spanned the United States from Atlantic to Pacific. American western expansion and development, despite the disruptions of the Civil War, threatened the potential of a Canadian nation and in particular the stability or security of the colony of British Columbia.

In 1870, Canada's first prime minister, Sir John A. Macdonald, argued conclusively for the building of a transcontinental railway not only to bind together the far-flung colonies and territories but also to join them as partners in nationhood. Once again, it was the promise of the railway that encouraged another colony, British Columbia, to join Confederation in 1871 and extend the political reality of Canada from sea to sea. In spite of the early disaster of the Pacific Scandal, which felled Macdonald's government, and the less than efficacious direction of his successor as prime minister, Alexander Mackenzie, it was Macdonald, once again in office, who saw the incredible undertaking to its completion in 1885.

What distinguishes the celebration of the CPR's centennial is that it is being celebrated across the land on different dates and in different years. The laying of track, the arrival of the first train or the driving of the last spike—any of these will suffice for setting the day of speeches and the organization of the parade. Even more important is the fact that whatever date or event may have local meaning it will have the significance of beginnings and of change. What was begun as the opening of the West is a large part of both our history and our present: the change not only shaped the land and the people in an earlier time but continues to do so in the world of today.

This book is a tribute to great Canadians of vision and determination and to the untold thousands who realized their dream no matter how humble their role. It is also a part of the Glenbow Museum's recognition of the immeasurable importance of the transcontinental railway, through exhibitions, scholarly debate, publication and public education.

For a museum in the core of a great western Canadian city, straddling the rail lines that gave it life, what other undertaking could be more appropriate?

Duncan F. Cameron
Director, Glenbow Museum

During the preparation of this book and a related Glenbow Museum *Acknowledgements* exhibition, it seemed sometimes that everyone I met across the West had worked for or had a close relative who had worked for Canadian Pacific or one of its many subsidiaries. I met people who had worked on the railway, in the steamship services, hotel system and many other arms of Canada's largest corporation. This was not, of course, coincidence, for the story of the arrival and impact of the CPR in western Canada is the story of the modern west.

This book was conceived as part of a major public programme of the Glenbow Museum including an exhibition, conference and two books to introduce the public to the complex, all-embracing role of the CPR in the development of western Canada.

Many people and institutions gave generously of their time, expertise and resources, especially Canadian Pacific itself, which provided the major support for the programme organized by the Glenbow. Corporate Historian and Archivist Omer Lavallée, as well as James Shields, Cecil Halsey, Peter Hrycaj and David Jones at Canadian Pacific Corporate Archives in Montreal reviewed the early drafts and made appropriate recommendations, in addition to locating many of the photographic images. All this work was done while the CP Archives was making a massive contribution to the Glenbow exhibition, "The Great CPR Exposition." Kind help was also given by Earl Olson and Ralph Wilson of Canadian Pacific, Calgary, as well as by Ken MacKell and Ivor Petrak of CP Hotels. While Canadian Pacific was very helpful, the Glenbow Museum had complete autonomy in the preparation of this book.

I wish to acknowledge the generous help of Alberta Culture and the City of Calgary, whose continuing assistance to the Glenbow-Alberta Institute made this book and the related exhibition and conference possible. Much assistance was also provided by David Monaghan of the Canadian Railway Museum, Leonard McCann of the Vancouver Maritime Museum, Keith Cameron of the British Columbia Maritime Museum, Edward Hart and Jon Whyte of the Peter and Catharine Whyte Foundation, Dr. Frederick Thorpe and Dr. David Richeson of the National Museum of Man, John Corby of the National Museum of Science and Technology, and Robert Turner of the British Columbia Provincial Museum. Thomas Kirkham undertook a number of valuable interviews with CPR officials.

I appreciate the assistance given by Sue Baptie of the Vancouver City Archives, as well as by my colleagues at the Public Archives of Canada, the Provincial Archives of British Columbia, the Provincial Archives of Alberta, and the Calgary City Archives. Neil Watson of the City Archives contributed much support to the Glenbow Archives at a time when our staff was involved with CPR research, as did City Archivist Tony Rees.

The Saskatchewan Archives Board, Provincial Archives of Manitoba, Moose Jaw Library, Medicine Hat Museum, Interior Photo Bank of Kelowna and Notman Photograph Archives rendered valuable assistance. My special thanks to Dr. W. B. Chung, Mr. T. D. Kilpatrick, Mrs. Lilian Pangman, and Mr. and Mrs. Taylor Stoess, who loaned valuable original documents.

Last but not least, I wish to extend a particular acknowledgement to the many people connected with the Glenbow Museum, who made this book possible. The Glenbow Board of Governors and Duncan Cameron, Director of the museum, provided much appreciated essential support to the entire project; Barbara A. Tyler, Assistant Director (Programs), gave key direction and encouragement and reviewed the text, while providing overall direction in the preparation of "The Great CPR Exposition"; Hugh A. Dempsey, Assistant Director (Collections), contributed valuable insight into the process of writing; and Lois Irvine offered useful advice. Research papers prepared by Don Bourdon, Doug Cass, Eric Gormley, Jennifer Hamblin, Lindsay Moir, Mary O'Brien and Lynette Walton—respectively on the CPR and tourism, the petroleum industry, irrigation, Calgary, urbanization, early literature on the CPR, the coal industry, the Crowsnest Pass, ranching and the meat processing industry—were of great help. Doug Cass, Assistant Chief Archivist (Manuscripts), assumed many responsibilities to enable me to concentrate on this project; his help was particularly appreciated. Marianne Fedori undertook research and provided much useful assistance. David Finch carried out research relating to the construction of the CPR. I also wish to thank Barbara Lindsay, Annette Crawley and Tania Yakimowich for their help. Ron Marsh gave the best photographic advice and assistance, and Patricia Ainslie offered expert advice on works of art. Lindsay Moir and Catherine Armon of the Glenbow Library advised on related publications. Lindsay was also kind enough to prepare the index and proofread the galleys. Chief Librarian Emeritus Pat McCloy pointed out useful sources of information as he encountered them during his own research. Carol Smith gave advice about the form and content of the book. Rick Budd provided much inspiration for this book because of his enthusiasm for the entire Glenbow CPR programme.

Special thanks to Pat Molesky, who spent many hours typing earlier drafts of the text with much enthusiasm. Leona Befus, Judy McLinton, Suzanne Di Rocco and Bernie Koziol provided assistance with typing and by generally helping with my workload. I could not have completed this book and the balance of the Glenbow CPR project without the research, support, enthusiasm and patience of all my colleagues in the Glenbow Archives.

Georgeen Klassen, Assistant Chief Archivist, played a major part in the selection of photographs and in editing earlier drafts while she was also co-curating "The Great CPR Exposition." I cannot thank her enough for her contribution. My editor Ruth Fraser rendered assistance and encouragement in the preparation of the text. Finally, I want to record the great support and encouragement I received from Sue Stone and my parents during the months of intense work when this book was gradually assembled. All opinions expressed are my own and I alone, of course, am responsible for any errors.

Bill McKee

1: The Impossible Railway

To build a railway, the CPR had to carve a right-of-way through an untouched wilderness across the West. Here, the line in the upper Bow valley approaches the formidable Rockies in 1885.

The idea of a transcontinental railway, bridging British North America from the Atlantic to the Pacific, preceded the creation of the Dominion of Canada itself. In the 1840s, Britain's North American colonies in the East were well populated, but still restricted to the Atlantic coast, the basin of the St. Lawrence River and the northern shores of the Great Lakes. Immediately to the north and northwest, stretching from the eastern shores of Hudson Bay to the Rocky Mountains, lay the territory of Rupert's Land, which was the fiefdom of the Hudson's Bay Company. Distributed across this vast land was a minute population of Indians and fur traders, and only one small settlement located in the Red River valley. On the Pacific was another British colony, in what is now British Columbia, where there were but a few fur trading posts, most notably Fort Victoria, as well as a native population. In other words, to the west of Canada lay thousands of miles of wilderness occupied by relatively few people.

The Birth of an Idea

A number of factors kindled an early interest in a transcontinental railway and Canadian acquisition of these huge territories, in both Britain and British North America. In 1843, the British Empire had seized control of Hong Kong on the coast of China; this settlement was to become Britain's major source of tea, silk, porcelain and other oriental goods desired in Europe. Since the Middle Ages, Europeans had been seeking a shorter sea route to Asia through North America—the famous North West Passage—to reduce the costly expense entailed in bringing goods westward overland through Asia or by sailing around the southern tip of Africa. The failure of many explorers to locate a northwest maritime passage to the Orient around northern North America had virtually killed the age-old search. However, the recent appearance and growing popularity of the steam locomotive as a fast, efficient means of land transportation, first in Britain and then in Europe and North America, had a profound impact. Increasingly, dreamers, engineers, politicians and others became convinced of the feasibility of a steam railway across British North America, to serve as the key link in a new shorter and faster route between Britain and its colonies in Asia.

As early as 1849, a British officer, Maj. Robert Carmichael-Smyth, proposed a "Grand National Railway from the Atlantic to the Pacific." He had never visited the muskeg and rocky wilderness of the Canadian Shield, the immense grasslands of the North West, or witnessed the towering mountain ranges of the far West. With the confidence, however, of the Victorian Age, he stated that such a project would present few problems for the British nation which had triumphed over a famous bog, Chat Moss, during the construction of the pioneer Liverpool and Manchester Railway. Despite such naiveté, the route mapped by Carmichael-Smyth in his published proposal was surprisingly close to the path eventually selected by the Canadian Pacific Railway. Although his idea betrayed an obvious ignorance of facts and was not adopted, it and similar proposals initiated the concept of a transcontinental railway in British North America. The breadth of vision demonstrated by Carmichael-Smyth and his contemporaries is all the more remarkable, since it

preceded by several years even the Grand Trunk Railway, which would link only Canada East and Canada West (today's Montreal-Windsor corridor).

Several additional factors eventually combined to make the concept of a Pacific railway much more feasible and popular, particularly in Canada. The arable land needed to absorb the tide of immigrants coming to the colony was becoming increasingly scarce as midcentury passed, and many would-be settlers were moving to the United States, where abundant lands were promised. If Canada was going to thrive, if the businessmen of Toronto and Montreal were going to develop larger markets, and if Canada was going to attract immigrants, new lands had to be opened up.

Rupert's Land with its millions of unsettled acres was the obvious choice. Although it was held as a fur trading preserve by the powerful Hudson's Bay Company, the company's control over trade and virtually every other facet of life in the region was coming under increasing criticism. In Britain, the age of the great trading monopolies was on the wane, and many people were hostile to an extension by Parliament of the HBC's monopolistic licence to trade. In Red River, the only settlement in Rupert's Land, an increasing number of free traders and supporters of annexation by Canada were expressing hostility to the company. Finally, in Canada, which had for so long been indifferent to the North West, the need for more land and the ambitions of Toronto capitalists were kindling a new interest in the region. The Hudson's Bay Company was even accused of promoting the image of the North West as a virtual wasteland to discourage settlement in order to protect the fur trade.

In 1857, the Assembly of Canada dispatched an expedition, under engineer Simon J. Dawson and Professor Henry Youle Hind, to the Red and Assiniboine valleys to assess the practicality of an improved transportation link from Canada and the agricultural potential of the area. At about the same time, the British government sent a scientific expedition under Capt. John Palliser to judge the suitability of the North West for farming and the feasibility of a railway route to the Pacific.

The Canadian expedition confirmed the agricultural value of the Red and Assiniboine valleys. It also stressed the value of the North Saskatchewan valley or "Fertile Belt" for agriculture and a transportation route, though it did not travel deeply into that region.

Palliser, as the result of a much more extensive exploration, concluded that the North West could support a large population and suggested a railway corridor up the North Saskatchewan River valley and through the Yellowhead Pass. He also confirmed the widely held belief that the southern prairies or "Palliser Triangle" were a northern extension of the so-called "Great American Desert" and unsuitable for agriculture. Despite their restricted endorsement of the suitability of the North West for settlement, Hind and Palliser had widened interest in the region among Canadians.

Meanwhile, American settlers had been pouring westward. By 1846, the floodtide of American settlers into Oregon had forced

Britain to surrender that territory. Three years later, the advance of American settlement into the upper Mississippi River valley led to the establishment of the Territory of Minnesota, and the town of St. Paul quickly assumed a dominance over the trade of the upper Mississippi and Red River valleys. The growing influence of St. Paul in the economy of the Red River valley, particularly after a rail-and-steamboat service was opened, made Canadians increasingly nervous. Anglo-American antagonism, which flared during the American Civil War, heightened Canadian anxieties about the ultimate fate of the North West. The American appetite for expansion remained unmuted, and as the construction crews of the Union Pacific and Central Pacific companies approached completion of North America's first transcontinental railway in Utah, the **Daily Alta California** of San Francisco declared on 3 February 1869:

That the U.S. are bound finally to absorb all the world and the rest of mankind, every well-regulated American mind is prepared to admit. When the fever is on our people do not seem to know when and where to stop, but keep on swallowing, so long as there is anything in reach. To use a popular Californianism, we "go for everything that is in sight."

Rhetoric like this kept Canadian fears alive, even as Canada was on the verge of acquiring the North West.

Events were also moving quickly far to the west in British Columbia. The discovery of gold there in the mid-1850s, and a subsequent series of gold rushes, had brought many American miners into the largely unorganized British fur-trade territory. In November 1858, the governor of the Colony of Vancouver Island, James Douglas, confirmed British authority in the region with the establishment of the Colony of British Columbia. For the next thirteen years, despite the attractions of continued British colonial status or annexation by the United States, the inhabitants of British Columbia would gradually move towards a link with distant Canada. At the same time, the growth of British Columbia, as well as a continued interest in the acquisition of the North West, encouraged Canadians to believe that a transcontinental nation could be created.

Through the Fire

Following the establishment of the Dominion of Canada in 1867, the nation's first government, under John A. Macdonald, moved swiftly and acquired the Hudson's Bay Company territories of the North West in 1869. As part of its preparations for taking over the territory, the Canadian government had already initiated work on a water-and-road link between Fort William on Lake Superior and the Red River valley. Originally proposed by Simon J. Dawson, it was known as the Dawson Route.

Macdonald had a vision of Canada as a transcontinental nation, linked by a railway from coast to coast. In the summer of 1870, Canadian and British Columbian delegations met in Ottawa to negotiate union. Because of the very poor state of travel between the Pacific coast colony and Canada, the three British Columbian delegates had journeyed south from Victoria via steamer to San Francisco, and thence by the Central Pacific and Union Pacific and their eastern rail connections across the United States. If the three men had travelled across British North America, they would have gone by horse-drawn stage, canoe, Red River cart, York boat or even dog-sled. They must have considered the contrast between that kind of journey and the speed, efficiency and comfort of their American journey by rail.

In Ottawa, the British Columbian delegates were offered terms that far exceeded their expectations; in return for entering the Canadian federation, they were promised that the Dominion would initiate work on a transcontinental railway within two years and complete the project within ten. While British Columbia was to retain control over its public lands, it was required to surrender to the federal government a belt of land along the right-of-way of the proposed railway. No longer only the talk of dreamers, the Pacific Railway was now an official project of the Dominion of Canada. In July 1871, British Columbia entered Confederation, confident that a rail link with Canada was impending.

The federal government, eager to initiate this project of unprecedented size, had already appointed Sandford Fleming, engineer-in-chief of the Intercolonial Railway, as engineer-in-chief of the Pacific Railway Survey. Even before British Columbia joined Canada, his work parties had been searching for the best route through the mountains. The task was immense: to locate a viable route through 2,500 miles of rock and muskeg in the Canadian Shield, across virtually unoccupied prairie, and through the forbidding mountain ranges and narrow canyons of British Columbia. In his epic review of Canadian surveying, Don W. Thomson underlines the brutal environment that the surveying parties encountered:

The rugged land consisted of rock formations, uncounted lakes, unbridged streams and heavy forests cluttered with areas of formidable windfall. A wilderness of swamp and muskeg, insect pests, fierce summer heat and bitter cold all combined to test the utmost stamina and resourcefulness of the individual surveyor.

Despite these and other hardships, such as inadequate food and shelter, the surveys proceeded surprisingly well. By 1872, Fleming had chosen to push the projected railway around the north shore of Lake Superior, northwest through the so-called "Fertile Belt" of the northern prairies to the Yellowhead Pass. In April, his choice of this low and gradual pass was endorsed by the government and in the fall he embarked on a personal tour across the country. His companion, George M. Grant, noted their satisfaction with the Yellowhead.

Instead of contracted canyon or savage torrent raging among beetling precipices as half feared, the Pass is really a pleasant open meadow. So easy an egress into the heart of the Rocky Mountains as that of the Jasper Valley, and so favourable a pass as the Yellow Head could hardly have been hoped for.

Fleming's preference for a westward route from the Yellowhead via the North Thompson and Fraser rivers to Burrard Inlet was not unanimously supported. Walter Moberly, Fleming's first engineer who was supervising the surveys in British Columbia, advocated a more southerly route, via Howse Pass, to the same terminus in Burrard Inlet. Moberly's successor, Marcus Smith, supported a more northerly route, via Pine Pass, Bute Inlet, and down Vancouver Island to Victoria. Given the complex geography of British Columbia and the conflicting ambitions of Victoria and towns in the lower mainland to become the Pacific terminus of the railway, it is not surprising that the route and the selection of a terminus were matters of continuing controversy into the 1880s.

John A. Macdonald's efforts to bring the concept of a Pacific railway to reality were not restricted to Fleming's monumental survey. His government decided to try to persuade a private firm to undertake the project; to this end, it was prepared to provide cash subsidies and a grant of land in the prairie section. In 1871, a predominantly American group offered to build the line, but because of a fear that it was not committed to a truly Canadian line, the government was not enthusiastic. Montreal shipping magnate Sir Hugh Allan, supported by the same American capitalists, offered to assume the project. After extended negotiations, Macdonald endorsed Allan's group, but without its American backers. In February 1873, the Canadian Pacific Railway Company, headed by Allan, was incorporated, and he went to London to seek financing. The optimism was short-lived.

Two months later, the Liberal Opposition announced that it had knowledge of corrupt ties between Macdonald's ministry and Allan. Over the next few months, the Opposition and the press revealed Allan's substantial financial support for Macdonald's party during the 1872 federal election. Macdonald was astounded to see reprinted in the press several of his telegrams sent to Allan during the final days of the election, including the now infamous message: "Immediate, private, I must have another ten thousand. Will be the last time of calling. Do not fail me. Answer today." The parliamentary select committee created to investigate the matter found no direct evidence to suggest that Allan had been awarded the railway charter as the result of his contributions to Macdonald's Liberal-Conservative party, but the credibility of both men had been destroyed, at least for the time being. In November, Macdonald resigned, and the Canadian Pacific Railway Company died with the collapse of his government.

Perhaps, for Macdonald, his absence from power during the next five years was fortunate. His successor, Alexander Mackenzie, assumed office as Canada entered one of the major economic recessions in its history. The declining economy constricted government revenues, and Mackenzie and his colleagues had no choice but to approach the Pacific Railway project with caution. The Liberal government, believing that the original terms of union with British Columbia had been far too generous and ruinous to Canada, endeavoured to convince the province to accept a less costly, slower approach. British Columbia—angered that the surveys were still incomplete and construction had not started by 1874, and by the Canadian government's apparent abandonment of its commitment to complete the railway within ten years—considered secession.

Negotiations with British Columbia lagged, but Mackenzie demonstrated his commitment to a national transportation system on a less imposing scale. In 1874, the government passed the Canadian Pacific Railway Act, offering a subsidy of $12,000 and 20,000 acres of land for each mile of completed main line to any firm prepared to undertake the project. Rather than attempting to find a single company to build the entire line, Mackenzie chose to start construction on a piecemeal basis, beginning with improvements to the link between Ontario and Manitoba. In August 1874, a contract was awarded to railwayman and former Liberal MP Joseph Whitehead to prepare the grade for a branch line from St. Boniface south to the American border. This line was intended to connect eventually with an American line from St. Paul and Chicago. Eight months later, a contract for the first section of the main line, between Fort William and Manitoba, was also signed. Under this contract only 32 miles were completed west of the Lakehead, but it did signal the start of construction of the Canadian transcontinental railway.

Progress on these contracts was very slow. Struggling through the muskeg and rock of the Shield, the main line crept across seemingly bottomless bogs and had to be blasted and hacked through one rocky ridge after another. Incompetence on the part of contractors did not facilitate rapid construction. Whitehead took almost four years to finish the 63 miles of grade on the "Pembina Branch" south from St. Boniface. Finally, in the fall of 1877, Governor General and Lady Dufferin drove the first spikes to begin track-laying in western Canada. In October, Whitehead brought one of the first locomotives to the western Canadian prairies: it was named the **Countess of Dufferin** and rather presumptuously called CPR Number 1. It was moved down the Red River by barge from Minnesota to St. Boniface. In 1878, the government took a further step by finally selecting Burrard Inlet as the Pacific terminus.

By that time, however, Alexander Mackenzie had lost the confidence of a depression-wearied population. In September 1878, he was swept out of office by Macdonald, who returned to power preaching the need for a "National Policy": higher tariffs to protect Canadian industry, western settlement—and a national transcontinental railway.

Full Steam Ahead   Back in office, his enthusiasm stimulated by an improving economy, Macdonald moved to hasten the Pacific railway project. His Minister of Public Works Charles Tupper, who was responsible for overseeing all the railway work being undertaken with government funds, detoured the main line from Selkirk, where it was to cross the Red River, south to Winnipeg. This decision assured the rise of Winnipeg as the major city of the prairies and affected the rest of the westward routing of the CPR main line. In 1879, a contract was signed for the construction of the first 100 miles of track west from Winnipeg. Contracts were also signed with Andrew Onderdonk, an American engineer, to construct the difficult line between Yale and Kamloops Lake in British Columbia, through the rugged Fraser and Thompson canyons, a distance of 127 miles.

Macdonald, meanwhile, was not prepared to consider government construction of the entire transcontinental line. Chastened by its experience building the Intercolonial Railway linking central Canada with the Maritimes, completed far over budget, the government of Canada wanted to find a suitable group of capitalists, dominated by Canadian interests, to build the line. Macdonald was also determined to have an all-Canadian line, despite the opinion expressed by some that a route along the north shore of Lake Superior would carry little local traffic and be more expensive than a line south of the Great Lakes through American territory.

In 1880, after extended negotiations, the government signed a contract with a syndicate represented by George Stephen, president of the Bank of Montreal; Stephen's associates in the St. Paul, Minneapolis and Manitoba Railway, James J. Hill and Richard B. Angus; Duncan McIntyre, whose Canada Central Railway would become an important part of the Canadian Pacific eastern network; New York financier John S. Kennedy; and a representative for British and European financial interests. Another partner, though not a signatory to the contract, was Donald Smith, who would drive the last spike several years later at Craigellachie, British Columbia.

According to the contract, the government agreed to complete and surrender to the syndicate the Pembina branch line and the sections of the main line that had been completed or were being worked on, specifically those lines between Lake Superior and the Red River valley and those in British Columbia. In addition, the government promised to give the syndicate $25 million and 25 million acres of land "fairly fit for settlement." Stephen and his associates were granted extensive tax and customs concessions, and the new railway was to be protected for twenty years from any competition which proposed to place a line south of its main line and connecting to American railroads. Finally, the CPR was to be allowed to expand its system eastward, so that it was, in fact, a rail network from Atlantic to Pacific. In turn, the syndicate promised to complete the main line by building approximately 1,900 miles of track within a decade, and to equip and operate it "efficiently" and "forever."

Criticism of the terms was inevitable; the Liberals accused the government of fiscal irresponsibility and giving away the irreplaceable wealth of the West. Toronto businessmen, outraged that the Montreal business community had apparently captured control of the nation's future life line, belatedly offered to undertake the project for less funds and a smaller land grant as well as other

STARTLING AFFAIR IN LONDON!

Western Canada, personified as a young woman, is being sold into slavery by Prime Minister John A. Macdonald for the sake of the railway. Cartoon from **Grip** magazine, 31 December 1880.

concessions. However, Macdonald was convinced that the government had already achieved the best deal possible, and that the line would be completed on time and by an all-Canadian route.

On 16 February 1881, the Canadian Pacific Railway was incorporated and soon began revenue-generating operations by taking over the existing government-built lines radiating from Winnipeg. On 2 May, the CPR started construction westward. Despite Sandford Fleming's surveys and recommendations for a northern route via the Yellowhead Pass, the CPR began to consider a more southerly alternative.

For a company motivated by the need to keep costs to a minimum, and the equally pressing need to open the line as soon as possible to generate revenue, the advantages of the southern route were no doubt attractive. It would be at least 100 miles shorter and would cross far fewer river valleys. Also, the company may have been aware of the very large coal deposits in southern Saskatchewan and Alberta which could help fuel the railway and provide freight traffic. And according to botanist John Macoun, who had explored the West with Fleming's surveys, the southwest prairies were not always as dry as Palliser had presumed. Most precipitation was simply concentrated in the spring, and the area was well suited for growing certain crops and for stock raising.

Finally, the new company may have decided to avoid the North Saskatchewan-Yellowhead route because much of the land along it was already inhabited by speculators; the railway would have been forced to purchase or go around such properties, adding substantially to the already rising cost of construction. By choosing the southern route, which passed through virtually vacant country, the CPR would have greater freedom in the location of the route and the sale of rural and town lands.

Soon after incorporation, the CPR had dispatched Maj. A.B. Rogers, an American railway survey engineer, to search for a more southerly route through the Rockies and Selkirks. By the end of the 1881 surveying season, Rogers had discovered the pass in the Selkirk Mountains that now bears his name and reported that he was almost certain of locating a southern route through the Rockies by the Kicking Horse Pass. In 1882, the CPR received the government's permission to relocate its route to the south of the Yellowhead, provided the chosen pass through the Rockies would not be less than 100 miles from the U.S. boundary.

During 1881, the efficiency and pace of western construction did not match expectations. Hill, on behalf of Stephen and his colleagues, brought in William C. Van Horne as general manager to oversee the entire project. Van Horne, who had had extensive experience managing midwestern American railways, brought along John M. Egan, who became general superintendent of the CPR's Western Division. Committing himself to build 500 miles of line in 1882, Van Horne hired Thomas G. Shaughnessy of Milwaukee as general storekeeper, to ensure that all necessary supplies were available on time and where they were needed as the end of track stretched westward.

"End of steel" was an amazing sight: grading crews, track-laying crews and a gradually shifting supply train, which held rails, fish plates, ties, spikes, gravel, pilings, timber and other supplies. Normally, sitting on a siding near the end of steel, was a second train with additional materials. P. Turner Bone, who worked on the prairie and mountain sections, noted:

End of Track was something more than just the point to which track had been laid. It was a real live community, a hive of industry, in which teamsters, tracklayers, blacksmiths, carpenters, executive officers, and other trades and professions all had a part. They had their quarters on a train composed of cars loaded with rails and other track material, followed by large boarding-cars for the workmen, and by sundry smaller cars for the executives. This train was pushed ahead as track-laying proceeded; and at the end of a day's work, it might be three or four miles from where it was on the morning.

Construction halted for the winter in 1882–83 and resumed in the spring, periodically reaching a phenomenal pace. In June alone, 67 miles of track were laid. In late July, a record 6.38 miles were laid in a single day near Strathmore. By August, the line had reached Calgary and was moving towards the Gap in the upper Bow valley. Contractor David Shepard later recalled:

In fifteen months, commencing May 1, 1882, our firm built 675 miles of the Canadian Pacific railway from Oak Lake [Manitoba] to Calgary, in doing which there were moved ten million cubic yards of earth, and all of the timber and pilings used in building bridges, culverts and other structures in the road bed was hauled ahead from the end of the track and placed in the work before the track was laid.

During construction, the rough unballasted track was left to be levelled and improved by follow-up work gangs. As a result, the first train to pass over the new track offered a rough ride. Turner Bone recalled that in the summer of 1883 he was ordered to move by rail westward to the end of track.

We had planned to do some office work on the way, but—as the track had not as yet been ballasted—the train rolled and pitched like a ship in a choppy sea, so that it was impossible to do any draughting; and we had just to pass the time as best as we could. At times, following a clatter which sounded like broken dishes, as the car gave an extra roll, we could hear a burst of strong language coming from the cook. Thus we were not without entertainment on the way.

By the end of the 1883 season, the line was nearing the summit of the Kicking Horse Pass. Surveyors and navvies clearing the route for the rail bed found the work demanding and at times hazardous. A CPR surveyor, Charles Aeneas Shaw, remembered:

We had completed the location nearly to the Great Divide when some of the men who were clearing the right of way started a bush fire. It had been a very dry season, and there were piles of brush and timber all along the line; the whole valley was soon in a blaze. Our camp was in a small open spot near the Bow River, which at this point was quite wide and had a small island in it. So we made a raft and ferried over our blankets, some supplies and cooking utensils. Everything else at the camp site we piled in a heap, with wet tents and some earth on top. Then we swam to the island.

The fire burned for days. It was pretty hot, and the smoke was bad for a time, but we, our camp outfit and supplies came through safely, also our horses, which we had driven to a small meadow close to the river. But some of the men and teams working on the line were burned.

Meanwhile, construction gangs under Andrew Onderdonk had been pushing eastward from Yale in the lower Fraser Canyon. Because white labourers demanded high wages and were often undependable, Onderdonk had brought in thousands of Chinese workers from San Francisco and the region around Kwangchow, China. Rock crews had blasted tunnels and road beds from the sheer cliffs of the Fraser and Thompson canyons. Using the Cariboo Road and small paddle-wheelers, which were dragged upriver with the aid of gangs of Chinese workers, Onderdonk had supplies delivered along the route. To facilitate the movement of rails and other heavy supplies, he also built a line in the lower Fraser valley from Yale westward towards the Pacific terminus at Port Moody; this was completed in January 1884. Then a massive cantilever bridge fabricated in Britain was carried by rail from tidewater to Cisco in the upper Fraser Canyon, where it was erected by midyear. Onderdonk completed his government contract in 1884, and was then hired by the CPR to build eastward through Kamloops towards Eagle Pass.

The human cost of this demanding and dangerous construction project was terrible, particularly among Chinese workers. Men were caught in rock slides and collapsing tunnels, as work was pressed with sometimes undue haste. Others fell off bridges under construction far above the Fraser. Apparently more than 200 Chinese workers died during an epidemic at Port Moody in 1883. As there were no occupational health and safety laws, even government contractors like Onderdonk had little to fear from federal and provincial authorities. Both levels of government were representing a public—in the West, at least—who was hostile to the Chinese. At least 600 Chinese died during Onderdonk's construction contracts, a cost of four men for every mile of track.

Construction was also proceeding on the lines between Winnipeg and the Lakehead, as well as the section of the main line north of Lake Superior. The Port Arthur–Winnipeg line opened for regular passenger service in 1883. To promote public use of this portion of the rail route to the West and generate badly needed revenue, the CPR established a passenger-and-cargo steamship service on the Great Lakes. Passengers could now travel by CPR from Ontario to the Continental Divide, deep in the Rockies.

With the discovery of the Rogers Pass through the Selkirks, the way to the Pacific was open. Despite a late start in 1884 due to deep snows which lingered at the Continental Divide, construction moved towards completion. The work of carving a rail line through the mountains was filled with danger. Turner Bone recalled that when he was at the site of present-day Donald, where the CPR was to bridge the Columbia River, he witnessed the following incident.

The bridge to be built across the Columbia was the principal one which engaged my attention at this camp. It was a two-truss bridge and the piles for the pier connecting these trusses were driven from a scow, which was attached to a cable stretched across the river.

One day, while I was watching the piles being driven, I saw, approaching the cable, a raft floating down stream, with a man and a camp outfit on it. It was quite evident that this raft would get entangled with the cable, which hung low close to the water. The pile-driver crew shouted to the man on the raft to look out. Too late! The raft swept under the cable, and passed on, but minus the passenger and cargo. For the cable caught the camp outfit and sheered it right off the raft. With both hands gripping the cable, and one leg over it, he gave an exhibition of some rather odd gymnastics as he bobbed up and down in his struggles, half immersed in the water.

When finally rescued from his plight by the men on the scow, he turned out to be Greer, one of the subcontractors whom I had already met and knew quite well. Having finished a contract, he was moving his outfit to the mouth of the Beaver River where he expected to get another job. He thought that floating by raft would be the cheapest way to get there. But he hadn't calculated on the hazard of encountering a cable on the way.

Creeping across rugged mountain ranges, around sheer cliff-faces and above roaring torrents, the engineering and track-laying crews from west and east moved towards one another.

Triumph in the Gold Range

Construction of the main line had taken five years, half the allowable time. While the surveyors, engineers and tracklayers had struggled against the elements and the landscape across 2,000 miles, the syndicate had been close to financial ruin several times. Only with government loans, the company directors risking their own fortunes, and the perseverance and organizational skill of Van Horne and his colleagues, was the CPR able to survive.

At last, on 7 November 1885, at a brief ceremony at Craigellachie in Eagle Pass, Donald Smith (later Lord Strathcona) drove the last spike. By the standards of the day, it was a simple ceremony. When the Central and Union Pacific railroads had met at Promontory, Utah, in 1869, creating the first American transcontinental railroad, a gold spike had been used as the final link. In 1883, when the last spike of the Northern Pacific had been driven, that railroad had spent $250,000 to bring over 330 key industrialists and politi-

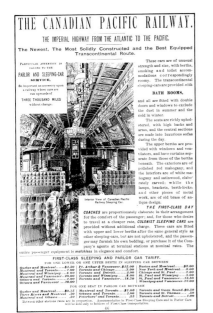

cians as well as the press on four luxury trains to the ceremony.

The CPR ceremony might have had some drama had the governor general, Lord Lansdowne, been able to drive the last spike as intended. Although he had had a silver spike made for the occasion and had travelled west in anticipation of the event, business had forced him to return to Ottawa prematurely.

In any case, Van Horne is reported to have stated, "The last spike will be just as good an iron one as there is between Montreal and Vancouver, and anyone who wants to see it driven will have to pay full fare." The small group that gathered at Craigellachie included Smith, Van Horne, Sandford Fleming, as well as John Egan and other officials. Tom Wilson, who was to gain fame as the first white man to see Lake Louise, had hopped on the train heading for Craigellachie, and peered over the crowd at Donald Smith. Symbolic of the hard-nosed approach of the CPR syndicate, George Stephen could not be present because he was in Britain endeavouring to capture the contract to carry the Royal Mail between the United Kingdom and Hong Kong, via Vancouver.

That same day near Donald, representatives of the men who had actually built the railway with their labour staged their own last spike ceremony.

In 1871, Pacific Railway Survey work parties began the immense task of locating a viable route through 2,500 miles of muskeg, prairie, forest and forbidding mountains. *(Left to right)* Frank Fleming, Sandford Fleming (engineer-in-chief of the survey), George Grant and Dr. Arthur Moren, 1871-72.

Another group of Pacific Railway Survey engineers.

A Pacific Railway Survey party portaging a canoe at Murchison's Rapids on the North Thompson River in British Columbia, 1871.

Geological and Pacific Railway Survey crew caching provisions and supplies at the forks of the North Thompson River, 30 October 1871.

Pages 28-29: In 1877, government contractor Joseph Whitehead had western Canada's first locomotive shipped by barge from Minnesota to the Winnipeg area. Later, this locomotive was named "The Countess of Dufferin" in honour of the wife of the governor general.

After the CPR decided on a more southern route than the original choice, the planned line was relocated from the Yellowhead Pass to the Kicking Horse Pass, near which this Canadian Pacific Railway Survey crew was photographed.

Construction westward across the prairies reached a phenomenal pace in 1882-83. Note the two-storey boarding cars for railway workers. These tall "hotels on wheels" were developed by American contractor David Shepard who built much of the prairie section.

A CPR work train unloads ties at the end of track. Most tasks had to be done manually or with the aid of horses. An intensive use of manpower and backbreaking labour was needed to push the line westward, often at the rate of three miles a day.

Before the CPR line began moving westward across the prairies, American contractor Andrew Onderdonk was building eastward from the coast to Eagle Pass in the Gold Range. *Top:* One of his crews assembling sections of a prefabricated cantilever bridge across the Fraser River at Cisco. *Bottom:* Another Onderdonk crew laying track in the lower Fraser valley.

In the meantime, other crews were pushing the railway westward through the Rockies and Selkirks. It was a slow, tough job. Often, the roadbed had to be carved out of solid rock, as shown here in 1884.

Westward-headed navvies blasting and hacking their way towards their meeting point with Onderdonk's crews at Eagle Pass. Meanwhile, construction continued in the rocky Canadian Shield section along the north shore of Lake Superior.

CPR construction workers. Although whiskey was banned in the camps, the man in the centre is holding a bottle and a shot glass.

On the north shore of Lake Superior, building stone abutments for a bridge over the Little Pic River, c. 1885.

Facing page, top: Dougherty's cut near Jack Fish Bay on Lake Superior.

Facing page, bottom: Crew at work near the west portal of Jack Fish Tunnel on the north shore of Lake Superior, c. 1885.

Temporary bridge erected on the north shore of Lake Superior for the use of work trains.

Pages 38-39: Members of the westward-bound construction crew, having crossed the continental divide, stand along recently laid un-ballasted track running down the Big Hill near present-day Field, B.C. Mount Stephen is in the background.

Navvies building an embankment cribwork to protect the railway
roadbed from the Kicking Horse River, 1885.

Top: Temporary towns like Beavermouth (winter 1884-85) appeared along the line during construction. Tents and primitive structures served as hotels, saloons and other amenities for workers. *Bottom:* Workmen on the Ottertail Creek bridge west of Field, B.C., 1885.

Pages 42-43: East of Rogers Pass in the Selkirks, high wooden trestles were built over rivers. This is the Mountain Creek trestle in 1885.

West of Rogers Pass at the famous Loops near Glacier House, 1885.
Left: The line was "S"-shaped to give it a gradual gradient, since a direct route would have been very steep. *Above:* Two sections of the Loops can be seen in this 1890 photo.

The last spike is home! The ceremony took place on 7 November 1885 at Craigellachie in Eagle Pass, where the east and west construction crews met. Donald Smith is driving in the spike; to his right are Sandford Fleming and William C. Van Horne.

A group of workers staged their own last spike ceremony at a point near Donald, over 100 miles east of Craigellachie. Visible on the left are two Mounted Policemen, always present to maintain peace during construction.

Artists in a Sea of Mountains

With the establishment of a transcontinental railway, travellers, including photographers and artists, could for the first time reach the West with relative ease and in comfort. To record scenic images along the line, the CPR actually commissioned photographers such as the Notmans of Montreal in 1884 and "Professor" Oliver B. Buell in 1885 and 1886. W.H. Boorne, R.H. Trueman and other photographers took additional views. Their photographs were used by the railway to promote a wider awareness of some of North America's most spectacular scenery.

During construction, engineers and other workers such as Herbert B. Lewis, H.O. Bell-Irving and Peter Turner Bone periodically paused to sketch and paint nearby scenes. After the completion of the railway, professional artists including John Fraser, Lucius O'Brien, T. Mower Martin, Marmaduke Matthews and Frederick M. Bell-Smith travelled west and, at times, were under the sponsorship of the CPR. Their work provided some of the first colour impressions of the magnificent mountain scenery.

Artists such as John Hammond and George Horne Russell were commissioned by the CPR to create very large landscapes portraying the power and immensity of the western mountains. These paintings eventually were displayed in major CPR buildings such as shipping offices, hotels and stations. Smaller sketches and paintings were used to illustrate and enhance CPR travel pamphlets and booklets.

Other artists who had no affiliation with the CPR also visited the West. Cleveland Rockwell's portraits of Glacier House and the Banff Springs Hotel show a delightful attention to detail, and Edward Roper's paintings include a human presence that was often absent in the works of his contemporaries, who were perhaps more impressed by the overpowering scenery.

The talented work of a number of artists and photographers helped the CPR to convey the glories of the Canadian Rockies and the Pacific coast to a very large audience.

"Puffing Billy" by Marmaduke Matthews, undated, painted near Mount Rundle which overlooks Banff Springs.

"A Tunnel, CPR Kicking Horse" by Edward Roper, undated.

Facing page: "Kicking Horse Pass" by Lucius O'Brien, undated.

Left: "Field, 1919" by Louis C. Tiffany.

Right: "Valley of the Loops, 1888" by Frederick Marlett Bell-Smith.

"Banff Springs Hotel, 1904" by Cleveland Rockwell.

Facing page: "Battle of the Rocks" by John Innes, undated.

"Glacier House, 1888" by Cleveland Rockwell.

Facing page: "Wings of the Morning" attributed to George Horne Russell.

2: Consolidating the Empire

Completing the main line was just the first step. Pacific-bound train at second crossing of Loop Brook west of Glacier. On the upper track is a second, shorter train.

Scheduled freight and passenger service opened between Montreal and Winnipeg on 2 November 1885, and on 28 June 1886, the first transcontinental passenger train left Montreal for the Pacific. Greeted with enthusiasm as it passed across the country, it arrived at Port Moody 139 hours later on 4 July. The "consist" or rolling stock component of the train included the luxurious dining car **Holyrood**, the sleeping cars **Honolulu** and **Yokohama**, and colonist, mail, express and baggage cars. As the **Pacific Express** rushed across Canada, rolling stock and engines were alternately dropped and picked up, so that little of the train that had left Montreal arrived on the Pacific coast.

In the mountains, reconnaissance and experience during construction had demonstrated that deep snows and avalanches could block the line, making regular winter and spring service extremely hazardous or impossible. During the winters of 1885–86 and 1886–87, the company established observation camps in the Rogers Pass, to record the date, location and size of the many avalanches that covered the tracks. As a result of their dramatic reports, the CPR decided to build over thirty snowsheds in the Rogers Pass section to protect the line. These structures had an aggregate length of more than five miles. Construction of the sheds began in the spring of 1886 and was completed after two seasons. Despite the prohibitive cost, Van Horne fully endorsed the snowshed concept. He did, however, insist on the construction of summer tracks outside the snowsheds to ensure that passengers did not miss the spectacular view of the Illecillewaet Glacier. Thereafter, year-round travel by rail was possible.

All along the line, crews were busy at the task of upgrading the road and improving equipment. Ballast was added to the hastily built road bed to give more stability and a smoother ride. Standard rail weights moved upward from 56 pounds (per yard) to 85 pounds in 1908 and to 100 pounds in 1921. Each improvement enabled the CPR to run heavier equipment, particularly locomotives, over the line. Rough wooden trestles were gradually replaced by fill, improved timber trestles or stone and steel bridges. In 1893, for instance, the 292-foot-high wood-frame Stoney Creek bridge, located on the eastern approach to Rogers Pass and reputed to be the highest railway bridge then in existence, was replaced by a steel arch span. In 1909, the CPR built a steel viaduct traversing the deep valley of the Oldman River (then called the Belly River) at Lethbridge, eliminating the long detour it had been forced to make on the southern Alberta Crowsnest Pass branch line. The new viaduct—over one mile in length, 314 feet high, supported by thirty-three towers—was, and still is, Canada's longest and highest railway bridge. Progress on such major projects was not without incident; three men were killed during the construction of the Lethbridge bridge.

Perhaps the most dramatic improvements made to the main line during its first fifty years of operation were three major tunnels—two blasted through the Rockies and one in the Selkirks—to eliminate excessive grades and curvature, and permit safer winter and spring travel.

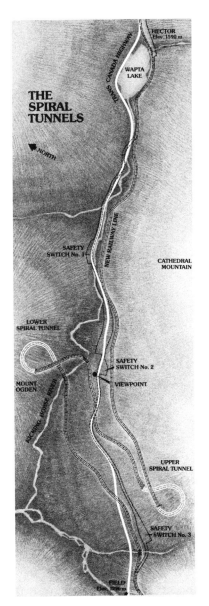

THE
SPIRAL
TUNNELS

NORTH

HECTOR
Elev. 1590 m.

WAPTA
LAKE

TRANS CANADA HIGHWAY

NEW RAILWAY LINE

SAFETY
SWITCH No. 1

CATHEDRAL
MOUNTAIN

LOWER
SPIRAL TUNNEL

KICKING HORSE RIVER

MOUNT
OGDEN

SAFETY
SWITCH No. 2

VIEWPOINT

UPPER
SPIRAL TUNNEL

SAFETY
SWITCH No. 3

FIELD
Elev. 1296 m.

In 1884, the CPR had won government approval for a very steep grade on the main line on the western slope of the Kicking Horse Pass; the so-called "Big Hill" was permitted as a temporary measure to overcome a particularly difficult engineering problem which would have delayed construction. The "Big Hill's" 4.5 per cent grade, rising four and a half feet every hundred feet, required trains to use specially built, very powerful locomotives; westbound trains were required to creep down the hill stopping to check brakes at each of three safety spur switches. Although accidents were rare, there are dramatic stories of runaway trains on this section of the main line. John E. Schwitzer, senior engineer on the CPR western lines, solved the problem posed by the "Big Hill" by adopting a tunnelling concept previously developed in Europe. The railway bored two spiral tunnels, the only ones in North America, through adjacent mountains; these tunnels with their approaches, reduced the main line grade to a maximum of 2.2 per cent. The famous "Spiral Tunnels" in Kicking Horse Pass were put into service on 1 September 1909.

In the Selkirks, frequent avalanches in Rogers Pass continued to make the line hazardous to use and expensive to keep open, despite the protection of snowsheds. The railway found the inconvenience of periodic closures to the line increasingly intolerable; the price of repeatedly reopening the line, the price exacted in railway workers' lives, and the hidden cost to the CPR while its trains were held up convinced officials that a radical change was required. A particularly tragic series of slides occurred in the spring of 1910 when more than sixty men were killed. This was followed by two more seasons of high avalanche danger. As part of a system-wide improvement programme, the company bored the five-mile-long Connaught Tunnel under Mount Macdonald, eliminating the section of the main line over Rogers Pass. The double-tracked tunnel was completed in December 1916.

As the years passed, Stephen and his successors gradually added more powerful locomotives to meet the growing demands placed upon the railway. Larger locomotives capable of pulling longer, heavier trains, however, called for heavier rails and steel bridges.

The "American-type" 4-4-0 locomotives used on the system in the early 1880s had weighed 45 tons and were capable of pulling very short consists. After Van Horne succeeded Stephen as president in 1888, he replaced these locomotives with more powerful 4-6-0 type engines. Between 1895 and 1900, 200 more powerful 2-8-0 "Consolidation-type" engines were added to the system for freight service. By the turn of the century, under T. G. Shaughnessy, the largest "Consolidation-type" locomotive in use weighed 98 tons. From 1905 to 1913, the CPR added over 500 class D-10 locomotives, a heavy-duty engine used throughout the system for everything from transcontinental freight and passenger trains to yard and work train service. By 1915, the CPR possessed over 2,200 locomotives. Under the direction of Edward Beatty, fourth president of the CPR, the company continued to expand its motive power throughout the 1920s. As prosperity peaked in 1929, it was introducing the 2-10-4 type "Selkirk," a very long, powerful locomotive which weighed well over 200 tons and was specially designed to pull massive trains over mountain grades between Calgary and Revelstoke.

The increase in motive power was paralleled by an expansion and improvement of rolling stock. During the early years of operation, the railway was swamped by spiralling grain production in the West and added many freight cars to try to cope with the rising demand. Although the number of cars rose from 3,072 in 1885 to over 9,000 in 1887, western farmers and rail critics denounced the system as inadequate.

The CPR opened its own shops for locomotive and car construction and repair in 1883. By 1904, to help answer the needs of its rail system and the growing demands of farmers, manufacturers and other shippers, it had added the 200-acre Angus shops in Montreal; by 1912, as Canada boomed, this facility was building 10,000 freight cars a year—30 per day. In 1914, the Ogden shops were opened in Calgary. That same year, the company opened the Transcona yard at Winnipeg to accommodate over 7,500 grain cars. Just before World War I, the introduction of steel to replace wood in railway car construction resulted in larger capacity and hence more efficient revenue operations. During this period, the quality and size of passenger service experienced parallel growth.

From the beginning, the CPR did not restrict itself to the travel and transportation business, and quickly assumed the role of a national communications system. Early on, Van Horne had advised Stephen to retain control of the commercial telegraph and express services; elsewhere in North America, these services were operated by independent companies, which leased railway facilities for such operations. Van Horne reasoned that since a telegraph system was required for railway operations, the CPR could profit from the system by operating it as a public communication service. Therefore, in 1883, the CPR opened an expanding national network. CP Telegraph's role in bringing the dispersed sections of the country closer together became especially clear during the North West Rebellion of 1885, when disaffected Métis and Indians rose against the Canadian government. The western telegraph lines, as well as the CPR line from eastern Canada, were used to maintain contact between Ottawa and its military forces in the West.

On Van Horne's advice, the company also established its own national parcel express service. Incorporated in 1873, the Dominion Express Company began operating under CPR control in 1882 and expanded westward with the rail line, providing the first scheduled, relatively efficient service for delivering small parcels between central and western Canada. In larger communities, Dominion Express vehicles performed the task on a door-to-door basis. In September 1926, it was renamed the Canadian Pacific Express Company.

At an early date the CPR became involved in steamshipping, a decision that had a profound impact on western Canada. In 1884, the company opened a passenger and cargo steamship service be-

The Marine Services of the CPR

tween Owen Sound and Thunder Bay. Three vessels, the **Athabasca**, **Alberta** and **Algoma**, were built in Scotland, sailed across the Atlantic, cut in half for movement through the canal system of the St. Lawrence and reassembled for the lake service. Just before the **Algoma** made her first voyage from Owen Sound, the local newspaper proudly announced:

No such vessels have ever been seen on the Great Lakes but their excellence lies not in the gorgeousness of their furniture or the gingerbread work of decoration but in their superiority over all other lake craft in model construction and equipment and in their thorough adaptability for the business in which they will engage.

In early May 1884, she left Owen Sound with more than 1,000 passengers destined for Sault Ste. Marie and Port Arthur. Because the CPR main line along the north shore of Lake Superior was still under construction, passengers transferred to the railway at the Lakehead and rode to Winnipeg and even as far as British Columbia. After the CPR rail line was completed around the north shore, this service continued to operate, providing an alternative link between southern Ontario and the Lakehead.

Although these steamers provided a dependable line of travel for tourists, immigrants, businessmen and freight, their record was at rare times marred by accidents. On the same day that Donald Smith was driving the last spike at Craigellachie, the **Algoma** was nearing Port Arthur in a high gale, with visibility almost eliminated by blowing snow. Suddenly she ran up on rocks; during the night she broke in two, some passengers remaining trapped on the afterdeck. The following day, the **Athabasca**, seeing distress signals, arrived to save the survivors.

In 1907, two more vessels, the luxurious **Assiniboia** and **Keewatin**, were built in Scotland and brought to the Great Lakes. Over 330 feet long, they had berths for 279 passengers. The passenger facilities on both steamers included a flower lounge with stained-glass skylight, a well-appointed dining saloon and a wood-panelled ballroom. Both vessels continued to operate on the lakes until the mid-1960s, when rising operating costs brought their end.

As early as mid-1886, the CPR was chartering vessels for the trans-Pacific trade. Four weeks after the CPR started transcontinental passenger service, the **W. B. Flint** arrived from the Orient at the Port Moody dock, with the first cargo of Chinese tea. In 1887, the CPR chartered three ex-Cunard liners, the **Abyssinia**, **Parthia** and **Batavia**, opening trans-Pacific passenger services. Before it could enter the costly trans-Pacific trade on a permanent basis, however, the CPR required a regular source of income to support each long trip. George Stephen had missed the last spike ceremony at Craigellachie because he had been in England lobbying for the Royal Mail contract across the Pacific. Finally, in July 1889, the company was awarded the contract and ordered three new steamers in Britain. At almost 6,000 tons the graceful clipper-bowed ships were nearly twice the size of the **Abyssinia**. R.B. Angus is reported to have been responsible for suggesting the ships be named after China, Japan and India.

In 1890, the luxurious **Empress of India** was launched, and sailed to Vancouver via the Suez Canal and east Asia. Arriving in Vancouver on 28 April 1891 carrying the first mail under the new Royal Mail contract, the **Empress of India** unloaded 131 passengers and a cargo which included tea and silk. She and her sleek white-hulled sister ships, the **Empress of Japan** and **Empress of China**, soon dominated the North Pacific passenger steamer business. By 1897, despite competition from eighteen other firms, the CP **Empress**es were carrying sixty per cent of all international first-class passenger traffic.

The design of these ships was bound to attract passengers. They were long, sleek and painted an elegant white. Although they were steamships, their graceful lines and the rigging they retained for emergency sailing made them very appealing to tourists. On the higher decks, accommodation was divided into first-class and second-class staterooms and cabins. There were luxurious dining saloons with delicately carved hardwood panelling, silk-lined walls and stained-glass windows. First-class passengers also had a library and lounge. Below deck, there was space for up to 700 steerage passengers.

In 1913, the CPR launched two more liners, the **Empress of Asia** and **Empress of Russia**, inaugurating a new level of service for passengers and cargo on the Pacific. Almost 600 feet long, each could accommodate nearly 300 first-class passengers, 100 second-class and 800 in steerage. The 21,000-ton **Empress of Canada**, launched in 1922, was 650 feet in length and was even more luxuriously appointed than her predecessors on the Pacific. She had a 110-foot "long gallery" panelled in Honduras mahogany, a verandah cafe at the stern, 30-foot swimming pool, gymnasium, bakery, laundry, hospital dispensary and barbershop.

The CPR trans-Pacific steamship service, extended from its Pacific terminus to Yokohama, Shanghai, Hong Kong and other eastern points, transformed the CPR from simply a national railway into a major link for Canada and Britain with the commerce of Asia. This was particularly apparent in the 1920s and 1930s, when the later **Empress**es operated in conjunction with fast transcontinental trains carrying silk.

The boom in coastal shipping that occurred in response to the Klondike gold rush convinced the CPR that a generous profit could be derived from an efficient, fast service. When the boom subsided, the CPR purchased the Canadian Pacific Navigation Company, the core of its new coastal waterborne operations. The sale of the fleet was consummated during a secret meeting held on board a CPR transcontinental passenger train; by the time it reached Vancouver, representatives of the Hudson's Bay Company, which owned a large share of the small fleet, had sold its interest to the CPR.

In 1903, the fleet was renamed the British Columbia Coast Service of the Canadian Pacific Railway. As the economy and population of British Columbia expanded dramatically between 1901 and 1911, the quality and size of the vessels in the Coast Service rose. The fleet of **Princess** vessels grew by ten new ships

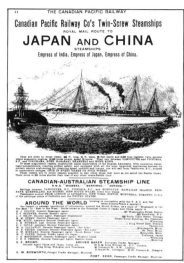

From the CPR booklet, **The New Highway to the Orient**, published in 1901.

during an eight-year period; they maintained a triangle service between Vancouver, Victoria and Seattle, as well as calling on points along the coasts of British Columbia and the Alaska Panhandle. They brought prosperity to the region and derived a growing traffic from most coastal communities during those years.

This expansion was not accomplished without incident. In October 1918, the **Princess Sophia** struck Vanderbilt Reef on the Alaska coast and sank in a driving storm with the loss of everyone on board, 343 crew and passengers. Despite such rare tragic accidents, the British Columbia Coast Service had a commendable safety record for decades, and was the life line for many isolated coastal towns.

Branching Out   As the railway worked its way west, settlers began to slowly fill the country. Better transportation was required to open areas away from the CPR main line if land was to be sold, settlement occur and the natural resources of the country developed. To answer those and many other needs, Canadian Pacific leased, acquired, or built main and branch lines from Manitoba to British Columbia; as a result, between 1888 and 1913 the company's total trackage rose from 5,186 miles to 11,366 miles.

Several of these branches are of particular interest. An entire network of lines provided rail access and encouraged settlement both south and north of the main line in western Manitoba. Much of this was built by the CPR, but important sections were built by companies later acquired by the CPR, such as the Manitoba South Western Colonization Railway, the Manitoba and North Western Railway and the Great North West Central Railway.

In 1891, the CPR-controlled Calgary and Edmonton Railway opened a line between Calgary and Strathcona, a town on the south side of the North Saskatchewan River across from Edmonton. In 1892, the line was extended southward to Fort Macleod. The CPR had acquired control of the line initially to ensure that the company and its land agents had access to company lands to the north of the main line; the southern extension performed a similar function, as well as drawing the southwestern ranching country into the CPR system. The development of this network, of course, ensured Calgary's role as the rail and service centre of southern Alberta, though Edmonton remained the capital city of the new province.

The extension of the Calgary and Edmonton Railway to Fort Macleod soon provided a connection with the new CPR branch line, which extended westward from Medicine Hat to the Kootenays. In 1893, the CPR leased the Dunmore-Lethbridge narrow-gauge coal railway originally built by the North Western Coal and Navigation Company in 1885, and converted it to standard gauge. The CPR was interested in the line because it provided access to an important source of coal, and could become the first stage of a line westward into British Columbia through the Crowsnest Pass, possibly extending to the coast.

After winning federal approval for a new line across the Rockies south of the Kicking Horse Pass, and receiving a substantial subsidy for construction in return for lower freight rates, the CPR started building the Crowsnest Pass line in mid-1897. Amazingly, it was completed as far as Kootenay Landing, with steamer connections to Nelson, in December 1898. As a direct result of the building of this line the huge coal mining industry of the Pass area began to develop.

Within the next few years the line was extended farther westward, other lines across the Kootenays and southern Okanagan were acquired, and the southern CPR route to the coast opened in 1915. Before reaching the Fraser River at Hope, the line had to pass through twenty-seven tunnels and bridges in a 30-mile section of the formidable Coquihalla Pass.

In the process of acquiring a line in the Kootenays, and as part of its struggle to limit American competition and reach the coast, the CPR acquired the Columbia and Western Railway, an event that had unexpected consequences. As part of the 1898 purchase the company was forced to acquire a primitive smelter at Trail on the Columbia River. Control of what was to become the Consolidated Mining and Smelting Company as well as the eventual purchase of the great Sullivan lead-zinc mine at Kimberley was to bring profits of unforeseen size after the discovery of an efficient means of separating the valuable ore components. Canadian Pacific's penetration of the Crowsnest Pass provided a link between the prairies and the coast, and established a strong Canadian corporate presence in the Kootenays. No longer would that country remain part of the hinterland of Spokane, Washington.

In 1905, Canadian Pacific also acquired control of the Esquimalt and Nanaimo Railway on Vancouver Island. Many islanders had thought the E&N would form the western end of the main line, but those hopes had of course not come to fruition, due to the difficulty of effecting a rail crossing from the mainland. Rather, the Island railway was built by coal magnate Robert Dunsmuir, with financial assistance from Charles Crocker, Leland Stanford and Collis P. Huntington of the Central Pacific Railroad in the U.S. In return, Dunsmuir received a massive land grant on Vancouver Island. Perhaps of greater importance to the CPR than the purchase of the E&N was its concurrent acquisition of the 1.4 million acres left from the original railway land grant. This land would provide valuable coal, timber and real estate revenues for decades.

During its first fifty years of operation, the CPR expanded immeasurably in the West. It upgraded its main line and extended thousands of miles of branch lines, increased and improved motive power and rolling stock, and diversified its activities. It was involved in national telegraph and express services, trans-Pacific and coastal shipping, mining, smelting and lumbering, as well as land sales.

Such dramatic growth and diversification was not accomplished without incident. Critics of John A. Macdonald claimed that he had been extravagantly generous with the terms in signing the original contract for construction of the line. Farmers and other westerners voiced repeated resentments against the CPR monopoly and freight rates, a controversy that still exists.

Railway Labour   Like many other industries in Canada during the late nineteenth and early twentieth centuries, the CPR was forced to develop a relationship with organized labour. Craft unionism had come to the Canadian railway scene long before the CPR was incorporated in 1881. The Brotherhood of Locomotive Engineers and Conductors had reached Canada in the 1860s, in the early years of the developing railway system of central Canada. In the following decade, the firemen and engine men were organized, and by 1876, ninety per cent of Canadian railway engineers were members of the Brotherhood. This early unionization occurred because the engineers and other crafts of the running trades had valuable skills, which enabled them to negotiate working rights.

As might be expected, the rugged conditions of CPR construction produced strikes by the construction trades, including trackmen. Some strikes were provoked by poor living conditions, as well as by the periodic nonarrival of the payroll. The early role of the North West Mounted Police in maintaining "perfect order" during the 1882 construction season was acknowledged by Van Horne in that year. On the other hand, in 1885, when the construction workers had not received their pay for some time, several strikes broke out in the mountains of British Columbia. At one point, the police were brought in to break up the strike and at least one worker was shot.

Railway workers continued to demand higher wages and greater job security, and one strike by trackmen against the CPR in 1901 played a particularly significant role in the evolution of labour relations in Canada. It led to the 1903 Railway Labour Disputes Act, which added a conciliation step to the process of bargaining. Several years later, the federal government implemented the Industrial Disputes Investigation Act, which brought further order to labour relations. Labour disputes continued, but the relations of the railway with the many craft unions gradually formalized as more unions appeared and negotiated contracts for their members.

The thousands of Chinese workers, who have become famous for their role in constructing railroads in western North America, worked primarily under Onderdonk between the coast and Eagle Pass. They were subjected to much harassment and paid very low wages for their work. At the end of their contracts, however, many were hired for permanent positions on the railway.

After the completion of the railway, a number of Chinese workers settled in British Columbia. Many returned to Victoria where there was a large Chinese community dating from the gold rush days. Others settled in New Westminster, for years the major mainland community. A number were also attracted to Vancouver, the Pacific terminus of the railway, whose rapid growth required the services of many newcomers.

By 1886, Chinese had also started to settle in major centres on the prairies, including Calgary, Medicine Hat, Lethbridge, Edmonton, Red Deer, Fort Macleod, Moose Jaw, Regina and Winnipeg. Because Onderdonk and his agents had brought only male labourers from China for the construction of the railway, and because subsequent Canadian immigration laws very tightly limited the immigration of Chinese women and children, many early Chinese camps and settlements were almost totally composed of males. Ironically, this development, which was intended to pacify white fears of the invasion of an alien culture, intensified them by reinforcing the distinctiveness of the Chinese community.

The arrival of Chinese in a town often provoked anti-Oriental agitation among local whites, who particularly feared lower-priced Chinese labour. At times this sentiment spilled over into outright violence against the newcomers. In 1887, a crowd attacked Chinese workers who were clearing the CPR lands of Vancouver's future West End, destroying their camp and forcing them to flee. The same crowd then turned on the Chinese community south of the old Granville townsite, burning several buildings and forcing the residents' temporary retreat to New Westminster.

Because of such hostility, the Chinese tended to concentrate in small enclaves along the periphery or in the cheaper districts of western communities, forming distinctive Chinatowns. By starting small truck farms and opening small service businesses such as laundries and restaurants, they became valued additions to many CPR towns. Sadly, these immigrants, who had been responsible for building with their own hands some of the most difficult sections of Canada's first transcontinental railway, were to face rigid prejudice for decades in western Canada.

On 28 June 1886, the first transcontinental passenger train left Montreal and is shown here arriving at Port Moody, B.C., on 4 July 1886.

Prime Minister Sir John and Lady Agnes Macdonald (*right*) at a halt near Mission, B.C., on their transcontinental trip from Ottawa to Port Moody in July 1886. This was no doubt a satisfying journey for the architect of a Canada from sea to sea, linked by the CPR.

Over the winters of 1885-86 and 1886-87, observation crews stayed in Rogers Pass to survey snowfall and avalanche conditions. This settlement at the Summit appeared during rail construction and was there in 1886 but was soon abandoned.

Avalanche activity in Rogers Pass made train trips hazardous if not impossible in winter, so snowsheds were built to protect the line at critical points. Interior of one of the 31 snowsheds, 1886. The immense size of the timbers indicates the strength necessary to withstand the force of repeated major avalanches.

Snowshed under construction during bitter cold weather on the east slope of the Selkirk summit.

Facing page: Once the line was completed, general upgrading began. This steel arch span replaced a wooden bridge over Stoney Creek, c. 1893.

As part of its upgrading—and to shorten the Crowsnest Pass line—the CPR began building Canada's longest railway viaduct across the Oldman River at Lethbridge, Alberta, in 1906. *Top:* Viaduct under construction, c. 1908. *Bottom:* An excited, courageous crowd of local citizens travel on flatcars in the first train to cross the viaduct on 22 June 1909.

An early mountain locomotive on the turntable at Field. These Baldwin-built 2-8-0 engines were kept at Field and Stephen specifically to assist trains going up or down the Big Hill.

Facing page, top: This early view—rare because it shows the entire consist of the train—was recorded near the continental divide, 1888. A pusher engine is located at the rear of the train. *Bottom:* On 11 April 1904, an avalanche crashed down on a work train, pushing these cars off the track just east of Albert canyon. Despite snowsheds, the danger of avalanches was very real.

Top: A rotary plow at work clearing the line in the Selkirks, 1914. *Bottom:* Steam-powered rotary snow plows, with powerful high-speed blades, could cut through deep packed snow better than regular wedge-type plows, but were not effective in clearing avalanches. Buried rocks and trees could damage the blades.

Facing page: To eliminate the cost and danger of running over Rogers Pass, the CPR built the 5-mile Connaught tunnel, a major engineering feat. This is the west portal under construction in 1914. It was completed in 1916.

Top: A 4-4-0 American-type locomotive used in the early days. The number describes the wheel arrangement: 4 small and 4 large driving wheels, no trailing wheels under cab. *Bottom:* In 1890, the CPR built three 4-4-2 Atlantic-type locomotives for high-speed eastern service, but on long-distance western lines, dependability was more important.

Facing page, top: In 1906, the CPR began to make larger, faster locomotives called Pacifics, with a wheel arrangement of 4-6-2 to support a longer boiler and firebox for increased power. *Middle:* Montreal Locomotive Works began making 4-6-4 Hudsons in 1929, with an extended boiler and firebox like the Pacifics. Tractive power was 45,300 pounds. *Bottom:* Also in 1929, the CPR designed the powerful new 2-10-4 Selkirk to pull large trains through the mountains. It weighed 453,000 pounds and had tractive power of 78,000 pounds.

Facing page, top: In addition to improving locomotives, the CPR built yards and work shops. The immense Transcona yards were established in Winnipeg to hold the growing number of grain and cattle cars. *Bottom:* Interior of a roundhouse in Penticton, B.C., used to service locomotives which traversed the rugged country on the Kettle valley line.

View of CPR shops in Revelstoke, B.C., strategically located to become a key service centre with locomotive and car repair facilities. Trains just leaving or about to enter the Selkirks changed locomotives and crews here, and had passenger cars serviced.

Facing page: Telegraph pole being raised in the Rockies, 1880s. While building the main line, the CPR extended a telegraph system across Canada to co-ordinate construction and train operations. Later, it carried commercial messages, revolutionizing the nation's communications and linking distant areas together.

Interior of a CPR telegraph office in the mountains of British Columbia.

Another part of the CPR empire was its trans-Pacific fleet. *Top:* The **Empress of India** is shown outward-bound from Vancouver harbour for the Orient. The famed "CPR style" was very evident in these elegant white ships. *Bottom:* The carpeted card room of the **Empress of Russia** with a grand piano and many vases of fresh flowers. *Facing page:* First-class dining saloon on the **Empress of Canada**, tables beautifully laid with linen, china and silver.

Without the backbreaking labour of thousands of workers, the CPR could never have been built or operated. These Ukrainian men were employed on line maintenance in the Crowsnest Pass, c. 1909. Many immigrants from southern and eastern Europe came to the Pass to work for the railway or in the area's mines and mills.

Workers burrowing under Rogers Pass on the construction of the Connaught tunnel.

Section crew in Beaver canyon. Each such crew maintained the switches and other components along a five- to six-mile stretch of track.

As part of its efforts to expand and improve services, the CPR built or encouraged construction of numerous branch lines, such as this one.

Boarding cars used during work on another branch line, the Calgary and Edmonton Railway, which finally brought the railway to Edmonton and tied it into the CPR system. It also strengthened Calgary's role as the economic centre of southern Alberta.

Laying track with the aid of a gantry on a CPR branch line near Castor, Alberta. Even into the 1920s, railway building continued to be a basically manual task.

Thousands of Chinese were brought to Canada to build the CPR. Here, a work gang upgrades tracks near Glacier, 1889. Those who couldn't get work on the railway after completion of the main line settled in or near towns in British Columbia and on the prairies.

Top: Man riding a velocipede, c. 1886-89. These light, single-person vehicles were used by CPR employees to make inspections or travel short distances.

Facing page: Living quarters of a caboose, 1905-06. These men set hand brakes from the tops of cars in motion and looked out for overheated bearings which could cause fires or derailments.

Bottom: Passenger train crew, 1911. The conductor *(right)* had charge of the train, ensuring compliance with schedules, operating and safety rules, and collecting tickets. The trainmen *(centre and left)* helped him and were under his orders, as was the engine crew.

Luxury from Sea to Sea

William C. Van Horne of the CPR took steps to ensure that passengers touring across Canada on the railway could opt to travel in relative luxury. In an early promotional brochure, **The Canadian Pacific: The New Highway to the East**, the company described its superior sleeping cars:

These cars are of unusual length and size, with berths, smoking and toilet accommodations correspondingly roomy. The transcontinental sleeping cars are provided with BATHROOMS . . .

The seats are richly upholstered, with high-backs and arms, and the central sections are made into luxurious sofas during the day. The upper berths are provided with windows and ventilators, and have curtains separate from those of the berths beneath. The exteriors are of white mahogany and satin wood, elaborately carved . . .

In its dining cars, the interior design, service and menus reflected a further commitment to quality. On tables adorned by stiff white linen and sparkling silver, regional delicacies such as Pacific salmon were offered to diners as trains passed across Canada.

Special trains containing luxurious private coaches with dining saloons and bedrooms were assembled for regal and vice-regal passengers. Some distinguished passengers such as Agnes Macdonald, the wife of Canada's first prime minister, periodically left the comfort of their private cars for the excitement of perching precariously up front on the locomotive's pilot to admire the spectacular mountain scenery.

Canadian Pacific's efforts were rewarded by a reputation for the quality and dignity of its services. The vessels it operated on the Great Lakes, across the Pacific and, after 1903, across the Atlantic, offered the same type of rich accommodation, dining facilities and service.

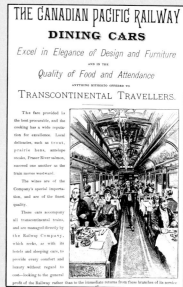

Pages from CPR brochures.

Facing page: Members of the 1901 Royal Tour by the Duke and Duchess of Cornwall and York pose on the locomotive's pilot beam.

Richly appointed first-class passenger parlour with comfortable individual armchairs, 1885.

A starkly furnished colonist sleeping car, showing some of the passengers reclining in upper berths, c. 1885.

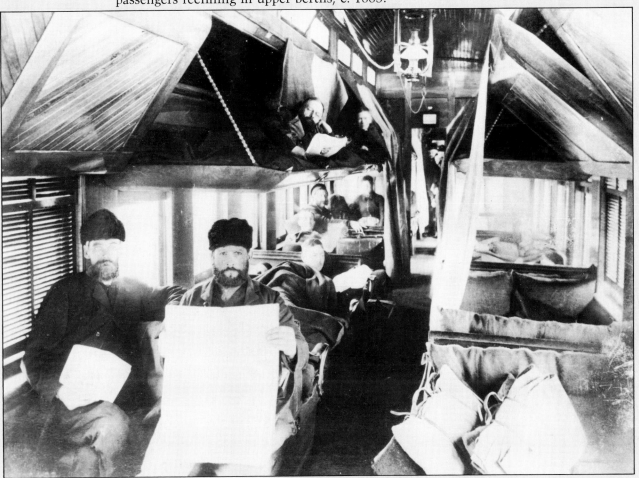

Pages 96-97: Interior of the dining car **Holyrood**, with white-uniformed staff members standing at back.

Dining room of the special car **Killarney**, which was used by the Prince of Wales on his tour of Canada, 1923.

Staff of the dining car **Tuileries** on the Royal Tour of 1901.

Bedroom of the special car **Killarney**, which was used by the Prince of Wales in 1923.

Interior of a CPR tourist sleeper, c. 1910.

Left: Interior of a CPR baggage car fitted up as a kitchen to feed British sailors en route to Esquimalt, B.C., 1890.

Right: Interior of the main room aboard a dining car on the "Trans-Canada Limited" passenger train, c. 1924.

View from a mountain observation car at the rear of a passenger train in the 1920s.

3: "The Wondrous West"

The railway opened up western Canada for settlement, dooming the old way of life. Blackfoot Indian sun dance camp in the 1880s.

Long before the appearance of the Canadian Pacific Railway, the native people and Métis had felt the effects of the move westward of the young Dominion of Canada. Even before its acquisition of the North West, Canada had sent surveyors to begin the task of mapping the region. When the surveyors reached Red River, they had ignored the existing river-lot system of land tenure used by the Métis and had imposed a land survey system based on a grid pattern. This insensitive treatment of the Métis, who feared the loss of their lands, was aggravated by the Canadian government's apparent disinterest in their concerns. Strident anti-French sentiments expressed by members of the small but growing contingent of Canadians were an added insult. Finally, a group of Red River settlers, led by Louis Riel, declared the establishment of a provisional government in the district. As a result of this action and some violence, Canadian forces under Col. Sir Garnet Wolseley were dispatched to the region to impose order. Although one Métis aim was achieved when the district became the province of Manitoba in May 1870, many disaffected Métis abandoned their homes and moved northwest to the fertile valley of the North Saskatchewan River, where they thought they could preserve their old way of life.

To these people, and to the Indians of the West, the railway's greatest impact was in its role as an agent delivering Canadian law and order to the region. With the arrival of the railway and telegraph system in the 1880s, the distant national government could shape and respond rapidly to events in the region.

When the Métis and some of the Indians of the North West chose to rise against the national government in 1885, again under the leadership of Louis Riel, the CPR, endeavouring to demonstrate its value to the nation, rushed the Canadian militia to the West across its uncompleted line. Transit time from the East to Red River was seven days, an impressive improvement upon the ninety-two-day trek required by Canadian forces over the same distance in 1870. The CPR telegraph system assisted in keeping Ottawa advised on the progress of the campaign. By helping to crush the rebels, the CPR played its part in the enforcement of Canadian law and order.

Later, in an effort to impress the Indians with its power, the government brought several chiefs to Ottawa by train. However, the Blackfoot were not intimidated. An interviewer summarized their reactions and cast them in the form of a speech by a character whom he called Apokena.

On my journey through the country of the white savages, I came to a big trail, which was made of iron . . . I stooped down and felt it with my hands. The iron trail was so heavy that I could not lift it, and the savages had fastened it to the prairie, lest some thieves come along and steal it. Whilst I was examining it, I heard a terrible noise like thunder, and . . . looked to see what had made such a hideous sound, and as I stood in amazement, there came another peal of thunder . . . down the iron trail came a fire-horse, roaring like a demon, and blowing great clouds of smoke out of his mouth . . . I saw the fire-horse drawing a lot of houses which sat on wheels, and there were many people in the houses. . . .

The Impact of the Railway on Métis and Indians

. . . I followed the iron trail . . . until I reached the place where the houses on wheels were standing . . . I went over to have a good look at the fire-horse. There was a savage throwing black stones into the gaping mouth of the monster, which it was chewing in earnest, and a great fire was roaring in its belly. After filling it up till it seemed satisfied, a chief shouted, and the horse ran along the iron trail to a house which stood high in the air and was full of water and the two savages gave it all the water it wanted to drink. . . .

. . . a fire-horse came along drawing some lodges on wheels, in which were a great many horses and tame buffaloes, and shortly afterward there followed another, with lodges full of people. The big travaille with horses and tame buffaloes had also some large trees and stones, which I supposed were being taken to the town to make lodges for the savages, as there are so many of them, that every day they have to make new stone lodges, as the savages are so cowardly that they are afraid to sleep on the prairie. . . .

Although the Cree had joined the Métis in the rebellion against the government, the CPR itself encountered limited resistance from the Indians of the West. In the spring of 1883, CPR surveyors appeared on the northern edge of the Blackfoot Reserve near present-day Cluny and Gleichen, Alberta. When they began to stake out the projected right-of-way of the rail line across what had until recently been reserve lands, unrest among the Blackfoot naturally increased. Crowfoot, a respected leader among the Blackfoot, complained to the local federal Indian agent, claiming the railway was trespassing on Indian lands. His grievance did not succeed, but rather than resort to force he agreed to allow the CPR to proceed.

Thereafter, Crowfoot and his people had little love for the railway, though—with help from him and Roman Catholic missionary Father Albert Lacombe—the Blackfoot remained at peace. He continued to press for compensation for the prairie fires on the reserve which were caused by sparks from passing locomotives and for animals killed by CPR trains, but met with no success.

William C. Van Horne had immense respect for Crowfoot, because of the peace that the Indian leader maintained between his people and the railway. In the spring of 1886, Van Horne had a pass for the Western Division of the CPR prepared for **Sapomaxicow** (Crowfoot's name in Blackfoot, as interpreted by the whites). Despite his sorrow for the continuing impact of the CPR and white settlement on his people, Crowfoot responded with dignity:

Great Chief of the Railway, W. C. Van Horne, I salute you O Chief, O Great. I am pleased with railway key, opening road free to me. The chains and rich covering of your name writing, its wonderful power to open the Road show the greatness of your Chiefness. I have done. Crowfoot.

Regardless of sentiments expressed by Crowfoot in his communication to Van Horne, it would be wrong to believe that the Indians were friendly to the CPR. After all, the railway had brought the forces to crush the rebellion, and they must have considered it an instrument to enforce white control of the region. Finally, the railway played a very active part in bringing settlers to the West, forcing the Indian people to retreat to their very limited reserves.

*Building
the Rural West*

The railway played a large part in the colonization of the prairies because it was a major landholder and needed to realize monies from the sale of land to settlers. Like earlier American railways, the CPR had built its line in return for large payments in cash and a grant of land. Because this land was to come from federal holdings, the grant was on the prairies where such land was available and "fit for settlement."

In the years following its incorporation, the CPR gradually selected massive blocks of land, consisting of alternate mile-square sections to a twenty-four-mile width on either side of the main line across the prairies. Odd-numbered sections were given to the railway and even-numbered sections were held for sale by the federal government, with a few set aside for school reserves and the Hudson's Bay Company. The CPR was not compelled to accept any lands which it judged to be unsuitable for settlement. As a consequence, much of its land would be located far from the main line. By the fall of 1882, only 5 million acres had been chosen, and the CPR had acquired its first large northern reserve, extending from present-day Saskatoon to the Rockies. It had also acquired a southern block of land straddling the western boundary of Manitoba.

Initial land sales did not meet expectations, and in 1883 the CPR sold 2.2 million acres to a British-dominated syndicate, the Canada North-West Land Company, a firm with close ties to the railway. The Canada North-West Land Company had obtained the right to purchase 5 million acres for $3 per acre; this purchase was to be accomplished by acquiring CPR land grant bonds valued at $13.5 million and then turning the bonds back to the CPR. The land company was, in effect, saving 30¢ on the price of each acre, but the CPR also benefited since the "sale" strengthened the market for its bonds. The land company also acquired half the land in all town, village and station sites from Brandon to the British Columbia border.

When the Canada North-West Land Company found that it could not raise the required funds, its contract was revised to cover only 2.2 million acres, as well as the townsites. Land sales lagged, however, and the company was liquidated in 1893. A new firm under the same name was organized, and the CPR quickly acquired control of it. With that step, the Canada North-West Land Company became a section of the CPR empire.

Despite the CPR's desire to sell lands, not only as a source of revenue to offset construction expenses but also to settle the territory and provide needed traffic, repeated crop failures and an extended depression inhibited immigration and land sales for many decades. In an effort to remedy the situation, the CPR established an Immigration Department under Alexander Begg. Maps, posters and

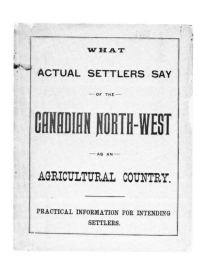

WHAT

ACTUAL SETTLERS SAY

— OF THE —

CANADIAN NORTH-WEST

— AS AN —

AGRICULTURAL COUNTRY.

PRACTICAL INFORMATION FOR INTENDING
SETTLERS.

From **Calgary, Alberta**, a brochure
published in 1885.

brochures promoting the Canadian West as a growing, healthy centre of agriculture were distributed in at least ten languages across Britain and northern Europe. To counter criticism and ignorance of the North West, Begg issued some brochures that provided testimonials from western settlers, such as **Plain Facts and Practical Hints from Farmers in the Canadian Northwest** and **What Settlers Say About Manitoba and the Northwest Territory**.

Towards the end of the 1890s, conditions began to improve. The Klondike gold rush influenced the revival of the world economy. Wheat prices began to rise and this, combined with the first widespread use of Red Fife wheat (which could mature during the shorter western Canadian growing season), instilled confidence and brought an increasing flow of settlers onto the land. Finally, the new Liberal government of Wilfrid Laurier began to actively support western development and immigration. Clifford Sifton, the energetic minister of the Interior from 1896 to 1905, established an ambitious immigration promotion campaign.

During the 1890s the combined efforts of the government and the CPR proved very effective. By 1903, the volume of immigrant traffic reached such levels that the CPR acquired its own transAtlantic fleet. During the boom which lasted until about 1912, the CPR's campaign in Britain included touring trailers displaying examples of the bountiful harvests of the West. The company also commissioned and distributed short films which graphically portrayed life in the West. The First World War virtually halted immigration from 1914 to 1918. With the return of peace, the immigration campaigns started once more. As a result of this long-term effort to attract people from Britain, the prairie provinces as well as British Columbia had a large population of Scottish, English and Irish settlers.

Beginning in the late 1890s, the company and government embarked on a similar prolonged campaign to promote settlement from the United States. Agencies were established, particularly in the midwestern states, to encourage farmers and others to relocate north of the line, and the literature distributed to them proclaimed the bounty of the Canadian West: **The Last Best West**, **Home Building in Canada**, **The Wondrous West**, **Canada, Land of Opportunity**, **Prosperity Follows Settlement** and **Evolution of the Prairie by the Plow** were some of the titles. The CPR funded excursions by newspaper editors, subsidized tours by prospective settlers, and worked with a number of colonization companies to sell substantial tracts of land.

Consistent efforts were also made to attract non-English-speaking immigrants, preferably in cohesive groups so that the members would provide each other with support, particularly during the tough early years. In 1885, CPR agents brought Hungarian nobleman Count Paul O. Esterhazy, who had been living in the United States, to look at land in the Canadian West. As a result of that initiative, 145 Hungarian families from Pennsylvania resettled near Minnedosa and at Esterhazy in the Qu'Appelle Valley. Of the CPR's role in this particular case, James Hedges has stated:

Not merely did the company [provide] *free transportation for all Hungarian immigrants from Toronto to Winnipeg, but through the kindly interposition of George Stephen, then president of the railway, financial assistance to the extent of $25,000 enabled the colonists to equip themselves with the cattle and implements necessary to begin farming operations.*

In the wake of these Hungarians came small groups of Icelandic, Scandinavian, French, Roumanian, German and Russian Jewish immigrants, who settled across the prairies. While many of them prospered, there were failures. When the German settlers at Dunmore, in the dry belt of southern Alberta, did not succeed, the CPR helped them to relocate near Wolseley and Grenfell, eastern Saskatchewan, where other settlers were prospering. However, despite the early optimistic expectations, by the later 1890s the West still had limited non-English-speaking populations. To encourage such immigration, after 1908 the CPR actively promoted community settlement by ethnic groups. Probably the most dramatic CPR initiative in promoting immigration in the 1920s was a campaign that brought 20,000 Mennonite settlers to the West from Russia. By extending credit to thousands of these people, who otherwise could not have afforded to finance their move and establish themselves on new farms, the CPR introduced to the prairies an industrious people who often settled in groups on large farms. Their tradition of community support for farming helped them to survive the difficult early years, when other isolated, individual families with no comparable support system were having problems. Mennonite farming traditions also led them to introduce a more intensive, diversified form of farming than that practised by many of their neighbours, who tended to rely on grain production.

In addition to encouraging settlement, the CPR promoted crop growing and stock raising appropriate to the existing climatic conditions, in order to establish a stable economy that would result in long-term traffic for the railway. In 1882, the company issued a circular announcing its willingness to "transport seed wheat westward free of charge, provided it is unmixed dark Scotch Fife." Very quickly, the CPR understood the value of the harder variety of wheat which matured quickly in the West's shorter growing season. Farmers who could grow wheat crops confidently, with less risk of frost damage, would provide a more secure, predictable traffic for the railway. As part of the process of determining whether the Palliser Triangle was indeed "fit for settlement" and to help identify the best crops and growing techniques, the CPR estalished ten experimental farms in southeastern Alberta. Because these studies were being undertaken across the dry belt, the CPR's land department did not initially select much of the land to which it was entitled along the main line in this region. James Hedges, in his epic study **Building the Canadian West**, states:

In doing a service to the company, these farms may also have rendered a kindness to numberless settlers, for had the railway

Hajtani.	Driving.
Ne hajtson gyorsan.	Don't drive fast.
Hajtson ki az országutra.	Drive out on the road.
Hajtson gondosan.	Drive carefully.
Ne hajtson lassan.	Don't drive slow.
Hajtson a hegy felé.	Drive on the hill.

Lovak.	Horses.
Fogja meg a lovat (kanczát).	Catch the horse (mare).
Hozza ide a szürke lovat (kanczát).	Get the grey horse (mare).
Hozza ide a barna lovat (kanczát).	Get the bay horse (mare).
Hozza ide a fekete lovat (kanczát).	Get the black horse (mare).
Vegyje le a szerszámot a lóról (kanczáról).	Take the harness off the horse (mare).
Fogjon be négy lovat.	Hitch up four horses.

Page from a Hungarian-English phrase book published by the CPR.

CANADIAN PACIFIC IMMIGRATION AND COLONIZATION ASK US ABOUT CANADA

accepted these lands, it would, of necessity, have sought to sell and settle them, with the resulting heartbreaks suffered by thousands of farmers who followed in the wake of the railways into the land of semi-aridity in the United States.

Many of these early projects were conceived by Van Horne, who also endeavoured to improve the capacity of the railway to accommodate larger harvests. By 1884, the system could not accommodate the volume of grain being exported from the West. Even after constructing two terminal grain elevators at the Lakehead and opening a grain shipping service through the Great Lakes and St. Lawrence River system, the CPR was forced to store grain in boxcars and converted flatcars. The construction of additional terminal elevators, as well as additional grain cars, eased the problem. At the same time, Van Horne encouraged the development of vertical grain elevators along the CPR's western lines, so that grain cleaning and grading could be done before it reached the rail cars would reduce railway costs substantially, as well as enhance Canada's reputation for superior wheat and other grains.

In the very dry country between Medicine Hat and Calgary, the CPR also developed a massive irrigation system to transform the area from a marginal to a productive agricultural zone. In 1894, Van Horne decided to accept a massive block of land in this region as "fairly fit for settlement" because of its location adjacent to the main line and its irrigation potential. In 1903, the government finally turned over the block of 2.9 million acres, and by the following year work started on the section closest to Calgary. By 1909, there were 1,600 miles of canals and ditches irrigating the area. Late in 1913, the massive dam on the Bow River near Bassano, Alberta, was completed; connected to it were another 2,500 miles of waterways to serve the eastern section of the Irrigation Block. The wisdom of irrigation struck home during the drought of 1918. Dry crops in the Brooks, Alberta, area were total failures, while irrigated land, such as that of the Duchess, Alberta, colony brought excellent returns.

To further encourage settlement in the area, the CPR established demonstration farms, such as the one at Strathmore, where settlers could examine the standard procedures for farming in the Block. It also embarked on several schemes of assisted settlement to bring more people to the region. Those who preferred to do so could even acquire ready-made farms, where houses and barns were built, and equipment, seeds and stock supplied, so that the first years of farming were less arduous. Although the CPR did not achieve the level of mixed farming and animal husbandry that it had anticipated for this area, it had made the development of the region possible.

Western Alienation

Despite the fact that the railway had played such a major role in the promotion of western settlement, it had encountered criticism and resentment from many westerners from the first years of its operation. The greatest controversy focussed on the monopoly clause in the CPR's charter. According to the clause, the government promised not to permit a competitive railway to operate south of the CPR main line to within 15 miles of the American border for twenty years. The intent of the clause was to prevent competition from drawing away traffic and revenue from the young CPR to lines south of the boundary. Considering what a costly, risky business the Pacific Railway was, it is not surprising that the Stephen syndicate insisted on this protection.

Resentment against this monopoly, which many farmers claimed allowed the CPR to charge unreasonable freight rates, inspired Manitoba to charter a competitive rail line, the Northern Pacific and Manitoba Railway.

This and subsequent similar provincial charters were disallowed by the federal government, under pressure from the CPR, because they ran counter to the firm's charter. However, in 1888, the Macdonald government, with the consent of the CPR, eliminated the monopoly clause. George Stephen was prepared to compromise by surrendering the clause in return for a federal financial guarantee on the sale of land grant bonds. It is probable that Stephen was also becoming impatient with what he felt was unwarranted criticism and he was concerned with the rising tide of hostility in Manitoba. Aware of the decline in the value of CPR shares, partly in response to the uncertainty engendered by Manitoba's agitation, Stephen sarcastically remarked to the prime minister that the stock loss was "more than Winnipeg is worth with all the people thrown in."

After the cancellation of the monopoly clause, many more railways appeared in western Canada, struggling for a share of the market for moving grain to export points. Other railways sought to capture some of the mineral wealth of the Canadian West, particularly in the mining district of the Kootenays. Competition between the CPR and its rivals produced some curious incidents. For instance, when the CPR-controlled Nakusp and Slocan Railway reached the mining town of Sandon and built a station, employees of the competing Kaslo and Slocan line (controlled by the Great Northern Railway of the U.S.) wrapped a cable around the structure and dragged it into Carpenter Creek under cover of night.

During the first decade of the new century, as Canada's economy boomed and settlers flooded into the West in unprecedented numbers, the Laurier government even went so far as to charter competitive transcontinental lines. Between 1902 and 1915, the Canadian Northern Railway was extended westward to Vancouver. Between 1903 and 1914, the Grand Trunk Pacific Railway was built from Winnipeg to Prince Rupert, on the northern coast of British Columbia. Both lines generally followed the route through central Saskatchewan and Alberta that Sandford Fleming had originally proposed for the Pacific Railway. When the economy deteriorated just before World War I, traffic declined and both firms experienced severe financial problems; the federal government had no choice but to take them over. Together with the National Transcontinental, a line from Quebec to Winnipeg across northern Ontario, and

LET THE BIG CHIEF BEWARE!

Manitoba, personified as a woman crushed by the CPR monopoly, is about to stab "the Chief," Prime Minister John A. Macdonald. Cartoon from **Grip** magazine, 18 November 1882.

the existing Canadian government railway network in Quebec and the Maritimes, they formed the Canadian National Railways, which competed with the CPR for the traffic of the central and northern prairies as well as British Columbia in the postwar years.

Behind the western resistance to the CPR monopoly clause had been the widespread belief that, in the absence of competition, the CPR was able to charge unnecessarily high freight rates. Farmers compared the cost of moving goods in central Canada with higher CPR tariffs for the same weights across a similar distance in the West and were outraged. Claiming that competition held rates down in the East, they reasoned that it could do the same for the West. Considering the fluctuations in the price that farmers received for their grain, their desire for lower rates was understandable. On the other hand, in light of the costs of constructing the railway, the West's limited population and markets, and the fluctuations in traffic, the CPR contended it was providing service at a reasonable price. In 1886, it also pointed out that its revenue from freight per ton mile was less than that of its major American competitor, the Northern Pacific.

In subsequent years, continued western agitation resulted in an important alteration in freight rates, the Crow's Nest Pass Agreement of 1897. In return for government financial assistance to build a line from Lethbridge to Nelson, the CPR agreed to charge specifically reduced freight rates on many manufactured products transported by rail to the West and on grain going east to the Lakehead. Since the terms of this agreement were to apply in perpetuity, the railway found it increasingly expensive to transport grain as costs rose. Although the rates were allowed to rise during the latter part of the First World War and were suspended for a short time afterwards due to high costs, the Crow's Nest Pass Rates were not only reinstated but extended to apply to Canadian National Railways, which had not been a party to the 1897 agreement. The debate over "Crow rates" has persisted. While the government has provided the railways with subsidies to allow them to continue moving grain at a lower "Crow freight rate," the railways have pushed for higher rates. Farmers, on the other hand, have continued to endorse the lower rates which, they claimed, made grain farming profitable and competitive on world markets.

Before the CPR arrived, the vast herds of buffalo on which Indians depended for food had been wiped from the western landscape. Settlers, however, earned money by collecting and shipping buffalo bones to eastern plants to make into fertilizer. Here, bones are ready for loading onto a train at Moose Jaw, Assiniboia, in the late 1880s.

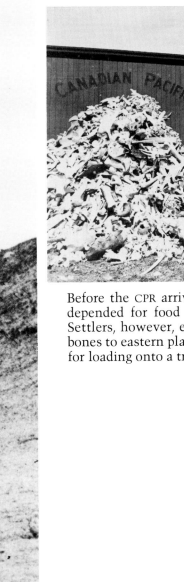

These Indians in southern Alberta were still living in tepees when the CPR built the Crowsnest Pass line in the 1890s. The Peigan and Blood people of the area found their reserves increasingly touched by the white settlement and agriculture encouraged by the railway.

When the second Riel Rebellion occurred in 1885, the as-yet-unfinished CPR proved its worth by rushing Canadian forces to the theatre of conflict in Saskatchewan. The Midland Regiment is on parade at the Winnipeg station en route to the front.

Facing page, top: During the rebellion, some Canadian forces remained behind at Qu'Appelle, Assiniboia, to guard this strategic transportation and communications point, 1885. *Bottom:* Crowfoot, leader of the Blackfoot Indians, played a key role in maintaining peace on the western prairies during and after construction of the CPR. In recognition of this, Van Horne gave him the rail pass he wears in this photograph.

Both the Canadian government and the CPR advertised widely to
promote immigration. In honour of the coronation of Edward VII in
1902, Canada raised this arch at Whitehall in London, England. The
arch, labelled "Canada, free homes for millions," is covered with a
mosaic of grains, fruits and different woods.

As part of the extensive effort to sell prairie lands, the CPR sent out exhibition cars to advertise the bounteous crops of western farmers, 1884.

Interior of an exhibition car, displaying examples of grains and other crops that could be grown in the West to dispell the still-widespread belief that it was a frozen wasteland.

Across the West, local real estate firms like this one in Stettler, Alberta, acted as agents for the sale of CPR lands—as well as those of the HBC.

Facing page, top: To further encourage western settlement, the Canadian government set up these colourfully decorated Emigration Offices in London, England. *Bottom:* Like the CPR, the Canadian government sent out exhibition vans. This one, which toured Britain, displays western wildlife as well as the usual sheaves of grain.

Symbolic of the diverse groups of immigrants from southern and eastern Europe that settled in western Canada by the thousands after 1900—in response to CPR and government campaigns—is this group of Doukhobors near Yorkton, Saskatchewan, 1902.

Concerted efforts to attract immigrants from the United States also met with success. In 1914, this "Solid Train Load of Settlers for Alberta" came from Colorado (where irrigation farming was common) to homestead near Bassano, Alberta, in the heart of the CPR's Irrigation Block.

HOUSE No. 6
BARN No. 1

Facing page, top: Departure of the train that brought the first group of Russian Mennonites to leave the Ukraine for the Canadian West. The scattered groups of people are the immigrants and their hosts, Rosthern, Saskatachewan, 1923. *Bottom:* One of the methods the CPR devised to help and encourage settlers was the sale of ready-made farms, complete with house and barn. Sometimes, seeds, equipment and stock were also provided.

Typical of thousands of British citizens who emigrated to Canada is this Welsh family aboard the Canadian Pacific steamship **Duchess of Atholl** in 1930.

This irrigation dam on the Bow River south of Bassano, Alberta, was built by the CPR between 1912 and 1914, as part of what was reportedly North America's largest irrigation project before World War I.

The agricultural potential that irrigation brought is evident in this 1915 photo. Potato cultivation was possible at the CPR irrigation farm at Crowfoot, Alberta, where crop growing had previously been very risky.

Harvesting rich fields of grain west of High River, Alberta.

The vertical grain elevators originally promoted by William Van Horne of the CPR to allow grading and cleaning of grain before delivery to the company soon dotted the prairie landscape. These farmers are hauling their harvest to elevators in Vulcan, Alberta, in 1928.

Lures to a Land of Hope and Beauty

When Canada acquired the North West from the Hudson's Bay Company in 1869, the region was little known and virtually unsettled. As late as 1872, explorer William Francis Butler had stated in his book, **The Great Lone Land**, "There is no other portion of the globe in which travel is possible where loneliness can be said to live so thoroughly."

The CPR faced the immense task of publicizing its vast new domains in the Canadian West in an effort to attract settlers, industry and commerce. In 1881, it published **The Great Prairie Provinces of Manitoba and the Northwest Territories**, which was directed at potential immigrants from Britain. An Immigration Department was established by the company in 1883 to lure settlers from Britain, northern Europe, eastern Canada and, later, the United States, with the aid of promotional maps, pamphlets, posters and advertisements. In addition, the CPR sent out agents and exhibition cars with samples of western produce to widen awareness of the agricultural wealth and potential of the West. Particularly after 1896, Canadian Pacific's endeavours were complemented by an aggressive campaign in the United States and overseas by the federal Department of the Interior to promote immigration. These combined efforts played a significant role in attracting a flood tide of settlers.

The CPR, however, was interested not just in settlement but in tourism. To that end, it annually issued pamphlets extolling the golden prairies, the glorious mountain scenery, and opportunities for climbing, fishing and hunting, as well as the fine service offered by its own trains. Dramatic posters promoted the pleasures of a cross-Canada tour via the CPR. Other firms took advantage of the situation by producing postcards and books of views illustrating the colourful highlights of the West along the CPR line.

The increasingly sophisticated advertising campaigns launched by the CPR to promote settlement, industrial development, commerce and tourism helped convert the Canadian West in the public mind from "The Great Lone Land" to a region of waving wheat fields and towering mountain ranges, inhabited by a hardy population of farmers, loggers and merchants.

Cover of CPR tourist brochure, 1890.

Covers of CPR tourist brochures published in 1896 *(left)*, 1894 *(centre)* and 1893 *(right)*.

  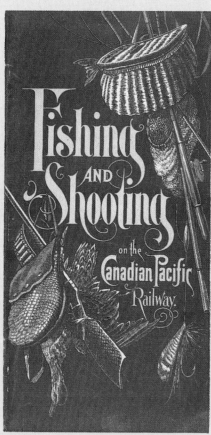

Facing page: Cover of CPR tourist brochure, 1909.

The Challenge of the Mountains

Cover of CPR brochure, 1921.

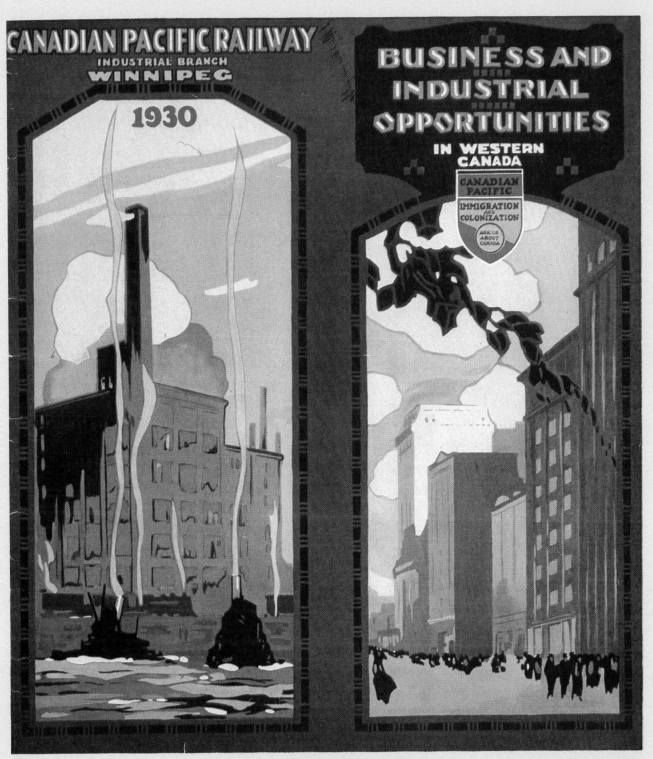

Cover of CPR brochure, 1930.

Canadian government poster, no date.

Facing page: CPR advertising poster, 1925.

TRANS-CANADA
LIMITED
SUMMER 1925
Commencing May 17
SLEEPING
CARS
ONLY
CANADIAN PACIFIC
MOUNT PALLISER
CANADIAN PACIFIC
PRINTED IN CANADA

4: A Frontier Tamed

As the CPR crept westward, it created towns and cities from the Lakehead to Vancouver, like this divisional point at Gleichen, Alberta, 1885.

Not only did the Canadian Pacific Railway play a major part in the settlement of the rural West but it also acted as the primary creator and builder of western Canadian towns and cities from the Lakehead to Vancouver.

In the course of his surveys for the Pacific railway in the 1870s, Sandford Fleming had made provision for the creation of towns at regular intervals along the main line. Since Fleming's towns were intended to provide services for, as well as gather the harvests from, adjacent farm districts, which used the horse and cart as their primary mode of transportation, he tentatively placed future communities only six to eight miles apart. In considering the needs of the railway itself, Fleming also recommended placing watering stations, engine-houses, and machine and repair shops at intervals of approximately 100 to 150 miles; such points would inevitably emerge as small population centres.

Once the CPR started surveying, grading and laying track across the West, it was faced with a unique opportunity to locate, create and shape urban centres on a massive scale. Furthermore, unlike many American railways, it was not compelled to accept specific blocks of land for townsites and rural lands, so the Canadian Pacific Railway retained an amazing autonomy in creating the urban landscape of western Canada.

Its decision to align the main line from the East around the north shore of Lake Superior, rather than inland, played a major part in the emergence of Fort William and Port Arthur (now Thunder Bay) as significant commercial centres. Two other company decisions ensured the long-term survival of the Lakehead as a major transportation centre: the establishment of a regular passenger and cargo steamship service linking the West with central Ontario via the Great Lakes; and the construction of large terminal elevators through which much of the West's bountiful wheat crop was shipped, rather than directing it all by rail to Montreal.

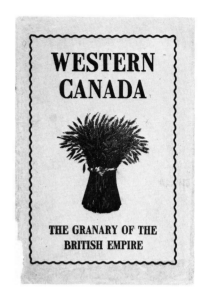

Early terminal grain elevators built by the CPR at Fort William.

WINNIPEG

In the Red River valley in Manitoba, the government's decision to divert the main line southward to Winnipeg killed the grand aspirations of Selkirk, which had been on the original route. In coming to Winnipeg, the railway encountered a community that had existed first as a fur-trade post and later as a small commercial centre and provincial capital for many years. Since the late 1870s, Winnipeg had had a direct rail link with St. Paul, Minnesota, then the economic hub of the northern U.S. plains.

The decision to shift to Winnipeg came in response to an enthusiastic campaign by the local Board of Trade and City Council, and the city's offer of a $300,000 bonus to assist in the construction of a rail bridge across the Red River. This decision was subsequently endorsed by the CPR. Furthermore, in return for a 30-acre site, a generous bond issue, and exemption from city and school taxes for twenty years, eventually extended in perpetuity, the company was induced to locate its main western shops in the city.

City Hall, Winnipeg

The effect upon the bustling but small community was swift and dramatic. The population exploded, land sales boomed, and the young city at the confluence of the Red and Assiniboine rivers spread out. Winnipeg's early industries had tended to locate along the Red for ready access to water transport, but the arrival of the CPR led to their relocation near the tracks. At Point Douglas, an exclusive residential area, there was a dramatic change in the landscape as industries and warehouses moved in, seeking access to the railway. By 1906, Point Douglas was occupied by lumber companies, saw and planing mills, foundries, agricultural tool and equipment factories, grain elevators and milling companies. The area also accommodated bag, tent and mattress factories and many other industries, as well as warehouses, hotels and government facilities, such as the Immigration Hall.

Because of its location adjacent to the railyards and industrial districts, Winnipeg's North End developed as a sprawling, working-class residential district. The poverty, ill-health, illiteracy and discrimination that were prevalent in the North End into the 1920s were a direct result of the largely ill-planned, rapid expansion the city experienced as the rail centre of the West. Winnipeg's emergence, then, as the rail, industrial, grain-trade and service centre of this immense region was spectacular, but not accomplished without social cost.

INSTANT TOWNS

Similar transformations were repeated in a more modest fashion across the CPR West, as the railway crept forward. Foreseeing the difficulties the railway would face in selecting station or town sites, Sandford Fleming had stressed in 1877 that "the station sites could best be selected in advance of settlement, before municipal or private interests were created to interfere with the choice, and when engineering principles alone need be consulted." He also warned that "the present opportunity would never again occur." As the line moved west, the CPR created over 100 towns and eventually 800 station sites. Historian W. Kaye Lamb summarizes the process:

Stations were located about eight miles apart; all had a 2,000-foot passing track, and in addition alternate stations had a depot, a section house, a water tank, and a 1,000 foot business track. Divisional points were established at intervals of about 125 miles—the distance a locomotive of the day could steam comfortably without refueling. Each had a train yard, an engine shed, and a coal shed, and every other divisional point had a repair shop.

Despite local idiosyncracies, the towns emerging across the CPR prairie west had many characteristics in common. The railway ran in a straight line across the centre of almost every town, and the station served as a focus of the community, since through it arrived people, supplies and news. The grain elevator, however, performed the major economic function in every prairie town, funnelling the grain harvest from the surrounding districts to the grain companies and co-operatives for delivery to the CPR.

Historian and geographer W. A. Mackintosh graphically defines the role that the railway played in these western communities.

The railway with its unfailing accompaniments, the loading platform, the two to five grain elevators, the post office, general store, machinery shed, and branch bank, closes the circuit through which the power of the world's economic organization flows into a pioneer community. What the birch bark canoe was to the fur trader, the railway is to the farmer of Western Canada. Beyond the end of steel there is only such settlement as waits month by month or year by year for the coming of the railway.

Following Fleming's recommendations, the CPR sought townsites where speculators or squatters were not already established, where the railway owned, could control or at least share the land and sale proceeds with the government, or where other more favourable circumstances prevailed. The choice of Winnipeg over Selkirk was a case in point. Several communities that assumed they would achieve city status once the CPR arrived were bypassed or ignored. For instance, at Brandon, Regina, Calgary and Vancouver, the CPR ignored existing or proposed settlements or districts and created its own townsites.

CALGARY

At Calgary, a Mounted Police post and distribution centre in southern Alberta, the railway chose to establish a station. Already the site serviced a broad district with trails to Fort Edmonton, Fort Macleod and Fort Benton in Montana Territory. Although a tent settlement had developed east of the confluence of the Bow and Elbow rivers in anticipation that it was to be the centre of the future town, the CPR established a townsite on its own land in August 1883. From that point, the small settlement of traders, cowhands and Indians quickly evolved into the commercial centre of the district.

As he had done across the West, Assistant Land Commissioner L. A. Hamilton laid out a rectangular grid townsite for Calgary. As usual, most major streets were named after CPR officials; main business blocks, hotels and government buildings quickly appeared along Atlantic, Stephen and McIntyre avenues, immediately north of the CPR station and tracks. Demonstrating their belief in the emergence of Calgary as a major regional centre, businessmen gradually replaced their wood-frame buildings with more imposing sandstone structures. The economy of the city expanded and diversified as business and industry arrived, attracted by Calgary's position on the main line.

The form and extent of this growth was profoundly influenced by the Canadian Pacific Railway. Most of the city's warehousing was built adjacent to the CPR tracks. With few exceptions, most of the city's limited industry located on the city's eastern periphery, adjacent to the CPR's rail line: Calgary Brewing and Malting, the stockyards and meat packing houses, the soapworks, and Calgary's first oil refinery (which opened in the early 1920s). The location east of the Elbow was especially attractive, since it was at the intersection of the CPR main line and the Calgary and Edmonton Railway. Grain, livestock and other goods could arrive from throughout the district, be processed and exported by rail to market very easily.

Calgary's residential districts were also defined by the CPR, which created subdivisions aimed at specific income groups. Mount Royal, the prestigious CPR subdivision developed on the city's south side after the turn of the century, was by design, and obviously by name, intended for the emerging elite of the young city. The Ogden residential subdivision for local CPR workers was developed on the southeast edge of Calgary, near the shops and somewhat isolated from the rest of the community.

Calgary's economic influence in the West began with the establishment of railway links between Calgary, Edmonton and Fort Macleod in the early 1890s, and was extended even further with the construction of the Crowsnest Pass branch of the CPR, into southeastern British Columbia. Although it did not dominate the economy of the Kootenays, Calgary could now service the area with relative ease.

Two decisions made by the CPR just before the First World War added immeasurably to the local economy and the status of Calgary in western Canada. In competition with Medicine Hat, Calgary convinced the railway to build major car and locomotive shops southeast of the city. The twelve-building complex, named Ogden Shops after I. G. Ogden, the CPR's vice-president of finance, opened in 1913 and occupied 213 acres. The 3,000 employees and their families meant an increase of 10,000 in the city's population, as well as the infusion of a very large payroll into the local economy.

In 1912, the CPR also took the first step in transforming Calgary into a major centre for the resource industries. It reorganized its operations relating to irrigation and colonization in the West into the CPR Department of Natural Resources. This new department, with its headquarters in Calgary, was responsible for the administration of the CPR's agricultural lands, timber resources, petroleum, mines, city property and townsites, as well as rural lands across the West. The Department of Natural Resources, in fulfilling these responsibilities, made Calgary's influence felt all the way to Winnipeg and to the interior of British Columbia.

VANCOUVER

Vancouver, the Pacific terminus of the CPR, was another rail and commercial centre forged primarily by Canadian Pacific.

Originally, the main line had extended only as far west as Port

Moody, which acted as the Pacific terminus from 1883 until 1887. However, the shallow harbour there, compounded by the presence of a number of squatters and speculators, made it a less than satisfactory site. Furthermore, in order to reach Port Moody, sailing and steam vessels were forced to negotiate a long passage from the Strait of Georgia through two narrow channels known for their treacherous riptides.

In 1881, a more appropriate location for the terminus had been suggested by Adm. G. H. Richards, on the "tongue of land separating English Bay from Coal Harbour." Van Horne visited Coal Harbour three years later when the CPR was negotiating with British Columbia over the possible move. He is reported to have exclaimed to his land commissioner, "Hamilton! Hamilton! This is destined to be a great city, perhaps the greatest in Canada, and we must see to it that it has a name commensurate with its dignity and importance, and Vancouver it shall be if I have the ultimate decision." Finally, in 1885, the provincial government transferred over 6,000 acres of Crown land near English Bay to the CPR; in return, the railway constructed a 12-mile extension of main line to Granville, a small lumber town near Coal Harbour at the lower end of Burrard Inlet.

In its characteristic manner, the CPR built its terminus station, dock, warehouse and hotel on the block of land it controlled west of the existing town of Granville, thereby creating the core of the future city. Abandoning the old Granville townsite, the federal post office and banks shifted to the CPR townsite.

After the arrival of the first through train from the East on 23 May 1887, Vancouver boomed, like many other communities formed by the CPR. The population grew to 13,000 by 1891. Industries, including foundries, sawmills and fish canneries, were established adjacent to the waterfront rail line. Receiving generous bonus and tax concessions from the city, American B. T. Rogers opened a major sugar refinery (using cane from the South Pacific), which distributed its products to eastern Canadian and foreign markets over the CPR route to Montreal. Additional industries that could not afford land near the railway were nevertheless attracted to Vancouver since the railway was at least accessible.

With deceptive ease, the CPR had created a major city and international port. The spectacular development of the company's regular trans-Pacific steamship trade after 1891, and of its British Columbia Coast Service after 1901, provided momentum to the emerging maritime city. To keep pace with all this growth, the CPR repeatedly upgraded its terminal facilities. As soon as it could, it backfilled the area between the company wharf—which looped out into Coal Harbour—and the high-water mark to create a yard for the increasing numbers of freight trains using the terminus. In 1898, the low wood-frame station was replaced by a more impressive "château" style, stone and brick-faced multistorey station. Between 1901 and 1911 the population grew from 26,000 to 100,000 and the new station was replaced by a much larger neo-classical building, reflecting the dramatic growth that Vancouver had experienced.

Following the establishment of the B.C. Coast Service after

1901, the limited CPR wharfage in Vancouver became totally inadequate for the quickly expanding fleet. The company therefore built a long pier, much of it covered by an immense warehouse, out into Coal Harbour. When the economy once more boomed during the 1920s and the CPR continued to add **Princess**es and **Empress**es to its fleets, even this pier became inadequate. The 650-foot **Empress of Canada**, or the slightly shorter **Empress of Asia** or **Russia**, could very easily congest the CPR dock. In 1927, the company erected an immense twin pier, 1,140 feet long and 331 feet wide. Around it extended 2,680 feet of berthage, able to accommodate five freighters, or two **Empress**es and a freighter.

Despite its role as the Pacific terminus of the transcontinental railway, and the fact that it was really western Canada's only major ice-free winter port, the full development of the Port of Vancouver had to wait until the 1920s. Cynical businessmen and government leaders refused to believe that Vancouver, isolated from British and European markets, could be a major port for the export of grain from the prairies. After a concerted campaign by H.H. Stevens, a local member of Parliament, the government finally built a terminal elevator in Vancouver in 1916, two years after the opening of the Panama Canal had shortened the distance to British and European markets. After a test proved that grain in bulk could be shipped with almost no spoilage from Vancouver to Britain and the Continent via the tropical Panama Canal grain began to flow through the port in large quantities. By 1923–24, exports of grain had risen to 55 million bushels from 500,000 twelve years before. It was only with this development that the true significance of the arrival of the CPR in Vancouver in 1887 became apparent.

The railway contributed as much to the size and shape of Vancouver's residential districts as it had to commercial growth. As the city prospered, the CPR gradually opened its lands in the area now known as the West End. In the years immediately preceding the First World War, the CPR initiated the comprehensive development of Vancouver's first specifically designed, elite residential subdivision, Shaughnessy Heights. This area, with crescent-shaped, paved and curbed streets, landscaped boulevards and huge lots, soon attracted the more prosperous citizens. Some of western Canada's most palatial homes were erected here. Abutting on Shaughnessy was the city's first golf and country club, a certain sign of the emergence of the CPR's western terminus as a relatively sophisticated community with a strong economic base. The similarity between Calgary's Mount Royal and Vancouver's Shaughnessy was more than a coincidence.

The Development of Western Industry

The story of the impact of the Canadian Pacific Railway on the rural and urban West cannot be understood fully without examining its role in the development of western industry. From Manitoba to British Columbia, industrial development, ranging from the lumber industry to the petroleum field to tourism, experienced the influence of the CPR or its subsidiaries.

LUMBER

During the years before the arrival of the CPR, the lumber industry in the West was mainly confined to coastal British Columbia. Although some logging had occurred on the coast and in the interior of the province in the 1850s and 1860s, it was on a limited scale to meet the local needs of the Fraser River and Cariboo gold rushes. Beginning in the 1860s, several very large sawmill operations were developed in Burrard Inlet to supply the unfolding markets for British Columbia's timber—the Hawaiian Islands, Peru, Chile, Australia, California and Great Britain. However, because of the lack of transportation to the rest of British North America before the railway, the mills of Burrard Inlet had limited their production.

With the arrival of the CPR, this situation changed dramatically. Existing mills were expanded and new ones opened to supply the immense demand of Onderdonk and the CPR for wood. The railway, after all, needed lumber for ties, bridges, snowsheds, stations, water towers and innumerable frame buildings.

During the late 1880s, lumber was also required for building the many towns and cities of the CPR, particularly Vancouver. Very quickly, the old Hastings Mill, located adjacent to the old Granville townsite in Coal Harbour, almost tripled its daily production, since it serviced the growing local community and was located adjacent to the CPR main line on which it could ship timber and lumber across the West. This expansion was mirrored at other mills.

The opening of the CPR's Crowsnest Pass line from the prairies to Nelson in the late 1890s meant that the Pass developed as a major sawmill centre to service the growing local coal mining industry, local towns and the vast prairie market. Fernie quickly emerged as an important lumber centre, with the first mill being constructed by the CPR at Coal Creek in 1899. Farther west, in the vicinity of Cranbrook, logging and milling also appeared on a large scale to supply mines, mining towns and smelters. The Crowsnest Pass Lumber Company plant opened in the East Kootenays in 1900 as part of this boom.

The arrival of the railway in the West, then, had a chain reaction; not only did it lead directly to the development or expansion of industries such as coal mining but also encouraged other industries such as sawmilling, which serviced the railway as well as the mining industry and western settlement generally.

RANCHING

Ranching had been developing in the western prairies and foothills since the early 1880s, in anticipation of the arrival of the railway, and as the result of federal lease regulations, which attracted eastern investment.

The arrival of the CPR was a mixed blessing for the ranching industry. While it helped to open the world to Alberta cattle, it also brought a flood of settlers who gradually intruded more and more on the ranch lands. The movement of settlers onto the range inhibited cattle ranching to such a degree that inventories actually declined between 1906 and 1909, from 900,000 to 600,000 head.

Although ranching prospered with access to the large markets of eastern Canada, British Columbia and Britain, the export of cattle was especially vulnerable to price fluctuations, changing import regulations and the price exacted by shipping live animals long distances. The cattle industry was also critical of the railway's service and complained about the inadequate number and design of its cattle cars. The CPR countered by suggesting that cattlemen simply needed to move their product to market over the entire year rather than all at the same time. Gradually, the establishment of feedlots, meat processing plants and reefers (refrigerator cars) assisted in the more orderly movement of beef to market.

Pat Burns, the most famous rancher and meat packer in the history of the Alberta industry, owed his rise in large measure to the CPR. He had started his career by supplying meat to eastern CPR construction crews and later supplied meat to gangs working on the Calgary and Edmonton Railway. Burns located his offices, slaughterhouses and stockyards at the hub of a network of CPR lines, so cattle could be received, processed and shipped to market with ease.

To encourage and assist the cattle and meat processing industries, the CPR established an animal husbandry branch in 1912 and offered many services, including the loan of sires, to local settlers. As another aid to improving herds, it also subsidized the delivery of improved breeding stock to the West. These services could be considered enlightened self-interest; a healthy industry would enjoy a good reputation and bring more traffic to the railway. The arrival and expansion of the railway, then, led directly to the emergence of meat processing and exporting as one of the largest components of the prairie economy.

MINING

With respect to the birth and development of the western Canadian coal industry, the CPR assumed an important but less direct role. Its arrival on the western prairies in 1883 inspired a syndicate to open a coal mine at Lethbridge and extend a narrow-gauge rail line from the mine to the CPR main line near Medicine Hat to provide coal to the railway.

The construction of the CPR through the upper Bow valley also precipitated the eventual establishment of mines and towns at Bankhead, Anthracite and Canmore to supply coal to the railway.

In the late 1890s, the Crowsnest Pass line was extended westward into the Kootenays, bringing about the development of coal mining ventures in both the Alberta and British Columbia sectors of the Pass. As part of its move into the area, the CPR signed an agreement with the British Columbia Southern Kootenay Coal Company to develop known coal deposits. Small mining towns, inhabited by a diverse ethnic population, appeared near the mines of this company and other firms. After the turn of the century, as the coal-fired economy of the West expanded dramatically and the appetite of the spreading western railways continued to grow by leaps and bounds, coal towns from Bellevue to Fernie—and beyond— prospered. Long lines of beehive-like coke ovens signalled the confidence of mining companies in continued prosperity. Imposing brick commercial buildings and hotels along the main streets of Coleman and other centres proclaimed the emergence of towns with plans for long-term growth.

Yet, this growth of the coal industry along the route of the Crowsnest Pass line periodically brought results that were unforeseen and tragic. In 1903, at least 76 people were buried when the side of Turtle Mountain crashed down on homes in the mining town of Frank, at the eastern end of the Pass. In 1914, at the Hillcrest mine, about one mile west of the Frank slide site, a series of gas and coal dust explosions killed 189 miners in one of Canada's worst mining disasters.

In spite of these and other tragic accidents, the wealth of coal in the Pass and the availability of railway transportation led to the development of one of Canada's major coal mining districts.

PETROLEUM

Not surprisingly, the CPR also participated in the development of the western Canadian petroleum industry, since it owned the mineral rights on all the vast lands granted to it. Crews working west during the construction of the railway had discovered natural gas by accident when they were drilling for water in southeastern Alberta. However, the discovery of oil at Waterton in 1902 provoked greater interest from the company, and its mineral rights reserve was extended to include petroleum.

Because of the extent of its land holdings, the CPR under its third president, Thomas G. Shaughnessy, adopted the policy of allowing others to take the risks proving up oil. For example, the CPR provided financial assistance to Calgary Petroleum Products Limited after its pioneer discovery of petroleum in Turner Valley in 1914. Drilling his third well for the Calgary company, Archibald W. Dingman had struck wet gas at 2,700 feet, which came in at a daily rate of 4 million cubic feet. Although the well caused a speculative oil boom in Calgary and made the city a regional petroleum centre, it was another decade before petroleum in commercial quantities was discovered. The CPR then provided more assistance to Dingman to enable him to pursue his search for petroleum in the area; if Dingman succeeded, the CPR, with its extensive mineral rights in the valley, would benefit.

Starting in 1919, the CPR and Imperial Oil initiated a very profitable relationship. While the oil company undertook the risk of exploring extensive blocks of CPR land, the railway simply waited and collected royalties on any discoveries. This approach paid off:

by 1925, the productive Royalite No. 4 well, which by its size ushered in the Alberta oil industry, had already paid over $50,000 in royalties; by 1930, royalty income from several lessees was almost $1,000,000. Playing a major but passive role, the CPR provided those who were prepared to assume the risks with access to the massive blocks of land that were required to locate petroleum resources.

Tourism

John A. Macdonald had considered the railway a matter of national policy—to encourage the development of the North West and to link the isolated sections of the country. Very soon, however, the Canadian Pacific Railway realized the profits to be achieved by promoting "on-board" tourism as well as tourist facilities in the more picturesque sections of country adjacent to the line. Railways generally were promoting more widespread tourism by offering a cleaner, faster and more comfortable means of travel than had previously been possible. The arrival of the CPR heralded the extension of the thriving, worldwide tourist business to the Canadian West.

William Van Horne visited the mountains and realized their tourist potential at once. He is said to have remarked, "Since we can't export the scenery, we shall have to import the tourists." To attract travellers, Van Horne convinced the CPR directors to build, maintain and operate the company's own first-class sleeping, parlour and dining cars. He also endeavoured to ensure that the quality of service on the system was superior; even menus were rotated so that local foods, such as salmon, could be served. The introduction and improvement of observation cars after the late 1880s allowed passengers to view the passing landscape, particuarly in the mountains, to a degree never previously possible. Finally, the introduction of tourist sleepers, a spartan option, opened rail tourism to far greater numbers of the general public.

Other improvements in rail service enhanced an already successful and popular system. In 1899, the CPR inaugurated the **Imperial Limited**, a transcontinental passenger train with an average speed of almost 29 miles per hour, dropping travelling time between Montreal and Vancouver from 136 hours to just over 100 hours. In subsequent years, even faster transcontinental train service was introduced.

By the turn of the century, new CPR branch lines and connecting steamship services had been inaugurated on the Columbia River and Kootenay, Arrow and Okanagan lake systems of the British Columbia interior to capture the agricultural, timber and mining economies of the region for the CPR. These auxiliary services opened new vistas for rail travel when the CPR made use of them for the tourist industry. At Revelstoke, passengers could leave the main line and venture by rail and paddle steamer southward to Nelson and vicinity, then travel east over the Crowsnest Pass route of the CPR. To cater to this tourist traffic, in about 1911 the CPR built a small hotel at Balfour on Kootenay Lake, where guests could go boating, fishing or hunting.

STATE-ROOM
IN
SLEEPING CAR.

Beginning in 1886, the CPR began to establish its first hotels in the picturesque country of British Columbia. Given the light engines of the 1880s, the railway decided that it was impractical to haul heavy dining cars across the high mountain passes. As a temporary measure, the railway made a practice of leaving its dining cars at strategic points, at the bottom of the Kicking Horse Pass and the west end of Rogers Pass. There trains halted while passengers took their meals. In their place, hotel dining stations were opened, the first being Mount Stephen House at Field in 1886. The following year, Glacier House was opened near the famous "Loops" in the main line, at the foot of the Illecillewaet Glacier in the Selkirk Mountains. A third such structure in British Columbia was Fraser Canyon House, at North Bend. Based on almost identical plans, the shingle-and-clapboard chalet-lodges provided excellent dining facilities for passengers and soon evolved into full hotels. All were attractive tourist destinations because of their proximity to beautiful mountain scenery, but Glacier House became a favourite with mountaineers.

In 1883, two CPR workers discovered a natural cave and basin fed by a hot spring in the upper Bow valley, at present-day Banff; and Van Horne later supported a request to the government that the area be reserved to ensure its unique character and beauty were not spoiled. He realized the tourist revenue to be derived from such a resource if it were handled carefully. In subsequent years, the railway advised the federal government of additional mountain areas that it thought should be set aside as parklands. Out of these early reserves emerged "Rocky Mountains Park," or the "Canadian National Park." This was Canada's first national park, later known as Banff National Park. Both Yoho and Glacier National Parks also had their origins in reserves originally proposed by the Canadian Pacific Railway.

Close to the hot spring, the CPR opened the Banff Springs Hotel in mid-1888. Accommodating 280 guests, it was one of the largest hotels of its day. This wood-frame, turreted structure was a luxurious facility for those who came seeking the waters of the hot springs. The richness of its accommodation and its magnificent location in the Rocky Mountains made Banff a major tourist destination. Designed by American architect Bruce Price, the Banff Springs Hotel was an early example of the "château" architectural style widely used in Canadian railway hotels, stations and public buildings for many years.

In 1890, the railway opened a modest chalet at the edge of incomparable Lake Louise, northwest of Banff. The chalet was much smaller and more rugged than its Banff counterpart, since it was designed to serve the mountaineering and hiking public. However, when the chalet was destroyed by fire two years later, it was replaced by a more commodious hotel intended to cater to the general tourist.

As the volume of tourists grew, the CPR moved to expand both the facilities at Banff and Lake Louise, as well as the hotel dining stations at Field and Glacier. By 1905, the Banff Springs could

Elevation plan of proposed chalet for the CPR's Swiss village near Golden, B.C.

accommodate 450 people, and by the summer of 1911 it was visited by no less than 22,000 guests. Between 1911 and 1928, the original wood-frame building was replaced by a more imposing steel and stone structure designed by W. S. Painter. In 1912, the hotel at Lake Louise was also expanded by the addition of a concrete annex designed by Painter. After another fire in 1924, the entire building was rebuilt in the more subdued château style of the 1913 annex.

In the years between 1898 and the First World War, the CPR continued to add to its hotel and lodge network. Tourist hotels were erected at Revelstoke, Sicamous and Balfour, and a lodge at Emerald Lake west of Field was opened. Mountain climbing in the Rockies and Selkirks became very popular and mountaineering tourists were based at Mount Stephen House and Glacier House. To assist these alpinists, the CPR brought mountaineering guides from Europe and even built a small settlement of Swiss-style chalets to accommodate them near Golden, British Columbia. The large financial investment required to initiate and maintain these diverse facilities indicated that, for the CPR, tourism had become a very big business.

Over the years, the CPR also developed a system of comfortable urban hotels aimed at commercial travellers, the local community and those tourists who were interested in going to town. In 1887, the CPR built a four-storey, brick-faced hotel in the centre of Vancouver. It was soon the social centre of the city and the residence of some of Vancouver's more prosperous citizens, including Mayor David Oppenheimer. The Hotel Vancouver was also a major tourist accommodation for people passing through the city and coming from or going to the Orient on the CPR's elegant **Empress**es. In later years, it was gradually expanded and replaced by larger, more ornate structures.

The "château" style associated with the mountain hotels as well as the CPR's Château Frontenac in Quebec City was not as widely adopted in the city hotels. In Winnipeg, between 1904 and 1906, the company erected the Royal Alexandra Hotel. Designed by Edward and William S. Maxwell, it consisted of a flat block, with ornate classical details on the exterior. Despite its rather plain outward appearance, the hotel had a luxurious interior and served as the social centre of Winnipeg for decades. Between 1911 and 1914, the railway built another block-style hotel, the Palliser, in Calgary. Designed by the same architects, it also had an ornate interior and quickly emerged as the focus of the city. In the late 1920s, the CPR erected a very similar hostelry in Regina, the Hotel Saskatchewan.

The Empress Hotel in Victoria was constructed on backfilled land in James Bay, donated by the city to induce the CPR to build the hotel. Adhering to the "château style" and offering superior service to tourists, the Empress could be reached by CPR **Princess** steamers from Vancouver, or via the Esquimalt and Nanaimo branch of the CPR, and played a major part in the emergence of the British Columbian capital as a significant tourist mecca.

Port Arthur on the Lakehead, 1885. The CPR made this town a railway centre and Great Lakes port, and built its first terminal grain elevator there. This photograph illustrates the pivotal role the railway and station played in towns along the line, with major business blocks and hotels clustering close to the station (behind the photographer).

At Olds, Alberta, a crowd protests the CPR's removal of a road crossing. This confrontation symbolized the powerful position the railway held in the West, since it alone chose townsites and crossing locations.

Winnipeg was for years the major station in the North West. The original station was built in 1882, gutted by fire in 1886 and rebuilt as shown here.

Main Street, Winnipeg, 1894. Its status as a western metropolis is evident by the many substantial structures and the streetcar system, just transformed from horse-drawn to electric power.

View of Calgary in 1889, six years after the arrival of the CPR. The photographer aimed his camera northwest across the Elbow River towards the centre of town, developed on CPR land.

Facing page, top: Calgary around 1911. Many commercial blocks, warehouses and storage yards have located along Eighth and Ninth Avenues where they are served by a CPR spur line. *Bottom:* In Calgary the CPR developed the elite residential district of Mount Royal. Many landscaped streets and mansions were like those in Vancouver's Shaughnessy Heights, a similar area created at the same time by the CPR.

Facing page: The beginnings of Shaughnessy in 1908. Shaping the forested wilderness into a sophisticated subdivision was not easy, as this view of the clearing operation illustrates.

An impressive home in the midst of Shaughnessy, built in 1912 by M. P. Cotton, one of the contractors who developed the district for the CPR.

CPR offices on Granville Street, Vancouver's main thoroughfare, 1892. Note the advertisements for its Columbia and Kootenay Railway and Navigation Company, as well as its steamships to Japan and China.

Facing page, top: In 1914, Vancouver's population was over 100,000 and the CPR built a larger station in the neoclassical style. On the left is Pier D, which provided expanded wharf facilities for the CPR **Empress** and **Princess** fleets. *Bottom:* The **Princess Patricia** of the CPR's coastal fleet, nearing the dock in Vancouver harbour.

C.P.R. Station & Docks, Vancouver B.C.

The New C.P.R. Flyer Princess Patricia Vancouver BC

KEEP CLEAR OF PROPELLERS

The CPR played a major role in the development of western industry by providing a means to ship products to markets. Here, a string of cars loaded with logs is being hauled to mills via the Kettle valley line.

Sawmilling was one industry, like coal mining, that also served the needs of the CPR itself. Two million lodgepole pine ties for the railway sit at Hawkins Creek near Yahk, B.C., c. 1928.

Ranching had begun in the early 1880s in anticipation of the CPR's arrival. Indians played a large part in the industry as cowboys, at work here on George Lane's Bar U Ranch, c. 1919.

By bringing rail lines into the heart of the southern Alberta ranching country, the CPR eliminated the need for long cattle drives and also encouraged the development of a meat-processing industry. Western cattle were shipped to extensive stockyards at Calgary or Winnipeg (shown here).

Left: The CPR's Crowsnest Pass line and its extensions brought about the development of many mining ventures in the Kootenays, such as the St. Eugene mines near Moyie, B.C.

Right: Construction of the CPR through the upper Bow valley led to the establishment of coal mines and towns like Anthracite, Alberta, to supply coal to the railway and the growing population of western Canada.

Men at work in the Trail smelter, which the CPR unwillingly accepted as part of a deal to acquire the Columbia and Western Railway in 1898. Later, the smelter was modernized as part of the Consolidated Mining and Smelting Company of Canada (COMINCO), a very profitable concern.

The CPR's steamboats and rail lines drew business to Kamloops, which became the main export point for cattle from ranches in the B.C. interior. In the late 1880s, the CPR line travelled down the town's main street.

To capture the Kootenay's agricultural, mining and timber economies, the CPR built branch lines and inaugurated steamboat services on the Columbia River and the Kootenay, Okanagan and Arrow lake systems. The **Okanagan** is visible from below the sternwheel of the **Sicamous** under construction at Okanagan Landing, 1914.

Pages 166-167: Given accessibility to markets, the fruit industry in the Okanagan prospered. A trainload of canned fruit in Kelowna, B.C., 1920. Teams of horses were used to provide the power for shunting the loaded boxcars.

In 1886, the CPR began to establish a network of hotels in major urban centres. *Top:* The first Hotel Vancouver built in Vancouver by the CPR in 1887. *Bottom:* Detail from an elevation plan of an addition to the Hotel Vancouver, 1901. Within a decade, the original hotel and this addition were being replaced by a high-rise, steel-reinforced structure.

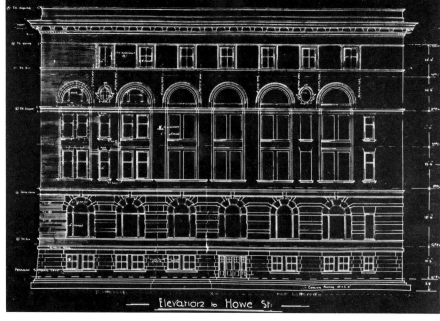

Elevation to Howe St.

Facing page: In Calgary, the Palliser Hotel was completed in 1914 and reinforced the city's position as an important regional metropolis.

The CPR was also involved in the beginnings of the West's petroleum industry. In 1914, Archibald W. Dingman *(front left)* discovered wet gas in Turner valley, causing a boom in oil stocks in nearby Calgary. The CPR gave Dingman financial help for further exploration, since it had extensive minerals rights in the valley and would benefit from any finds.

A CPR well at Brooks, Alberta, 1912. Normally the CPR allowed other companies to undertake the risk of exploration for petroleum on its vast properties, but it did periodically become directly involved in drilling.

Castles in the Wilderness

Canadian Pacific's commitment to providing a quality travel experience for its more affluent passengers extended beyond its onboard facilities to a network of small hostelries and grand hotels in the western mountains, as well as several notable city hotels.

In the summer of 1886, the CPR began building three mountain dining stations in the "Swiss chalet" style at Field (Mount Stephen House), Glacier (Glacier House), and North Bend (Fraser Canyon House), all in British Columbia. At these dining stations, trains paused while passengers disembarked to be served their meals, thus eliminating the need to haul heavy dining cars up steep grades. English traveller and writer Douglas Sladen described a stop at Glacier House in his 1895 book **On the Cars and Off**.

There is nothing of "twenty minutes at Normanton for refreshment" about a Canadian Pacific Railway dining station; the train just stops till the last passenger is finished. ... The second-class passengers, who came on board the train with knapsacks full of unsavories, usually lunched off – teasing the bears. The first-class passengers hurried through an excellent menu at the restaurant, and then had half an hour to dawdle about the platforms, gazing at the glacier ...

In 1883, the company opened the luxurious Banff Springs Hotel at a splendid scenic location in the Rockies, praising it as "a large and handsome structure, with every convenience that modern ingenuity can suggest, and costing over a quarter of a million dollars." A much less imposing small chalet was opened in 1890 on alpine Lake Louise northwest of Banff. Intended for the more hardy visitor to the mountains, who preferred to rough it, the chalet gradually evolved into a multistoried, reinforced concrete "château." Smaller hotels were also opened at Revelstoke, Sicamous and Kootenay Lake (the last two especially for hunters and fishermen), but it was the "Castles in the Wilderness" at Banff Springs and Lake Louise that became two of the most popular tourist destinations in North America.

Facing page, top: The "Pacific Express" stopping at Mount Stephen House in Field, 1886-89. *Bottom:* Interior of Mount Stephen House, 1902.

Top: Train stopped at Glacier House. *Middle:* Fully-set tables in the dining room of Glacier House, 1886-89. *Bottom:* As the popularity of Glacier House grew, the building was extended dramatically. Elevation plan of proposed extension, 1926.

Top: Glacier House staff in 1899, including Swiss climbing guides Edward Feuz and Christian Haesler. *Bottom:* Feuz and Haesler, the guides who led visitors on expeditions and promoted safe mountaineering. They were brought to Glacier House by the CPR to encourage the notion of the Rockies and Selkirks as a North American "Switzerland."

Top: The first small chalet on the edge of Lake Louise, 1890. *Bottom:* Staff at Lake Louise, 1904. This summer hotel replaced the original small chalet which had burned down.

A tally-ho service carried guests from the Laggan station to the hotel at Lake Louise. Note the new Rattenbury wing at right.

Top: This narrow-gauge tram replaced the tally-ho service in 1912.

Facing page: By 1913, the hotel at Lake Louise had, in addition to the Rattenbury wing *(left)* a new reinforced concrete wing *(right)*, as shown in this 1921 photograph.

Bottom: Rattenbury wing being destroyed by fire, July 1924.

Facing page: An early view of the Banff Springs Hotel in front of Mount Rundle.

Viewing veranda and band-stand at Banff Springs Hotel, overlooking the Bow valley, 1890.

Until after the turn of the century, the CPR continued to expand the original wood-frame hotel at Banff Springs.

The Banff Springs Hotel's north wing was destroyed by fire and replaced in 1926-27. In the latter year, construction began on the steel-frame replacement of the south wing.

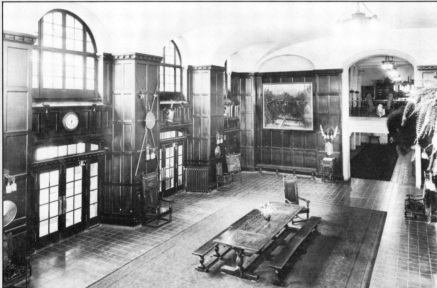

Rotunda of the Banff Springs Hotel.

A group of Stoney Indians, who were for many years a popular part of tourists' visits, in front of the Banff Springs Hotel, c. 1928.

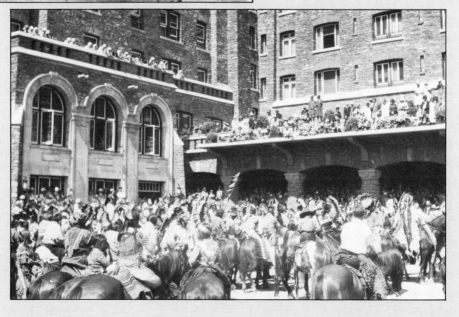

Epilogue

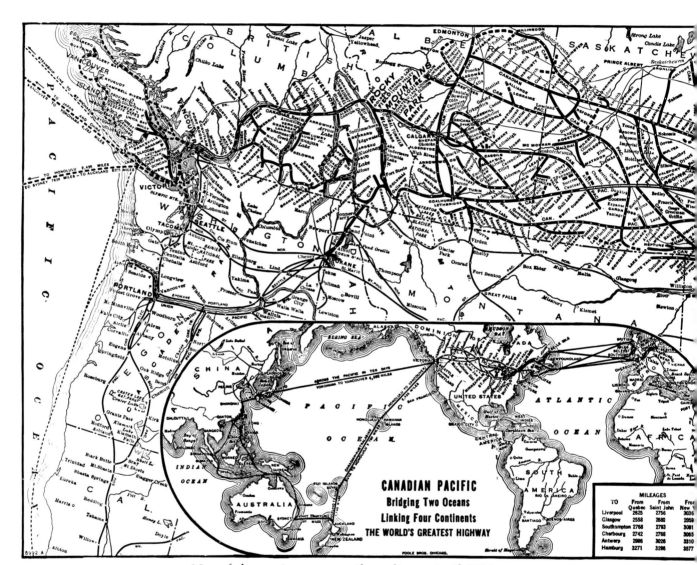

Map of the CPR's western railway lines, April 1929.

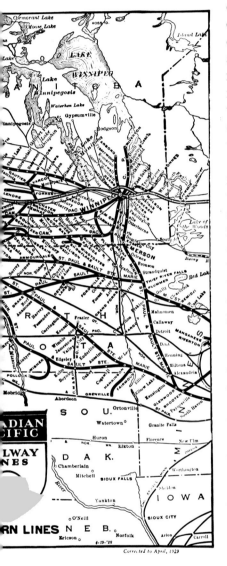

The story of the Canadian Pacific Railway in western Canada cannot be restricted to a description of the birth, construction and operations of the railway itself. More than any other human agency, the CPR shaped the development of most aspects of social, political and economic life in the West. Even as it was acting as one of the major instruments of national policy, designed to ensure the survival of the young Dominion of Canada, the railway had a more concrete effect upon the nature and direction of life in the West. Because of the diverse composition and immense power of the company, that influence was all-encompassing. It forged the dream of a transcontinental British North America into a reality by physically joining the distant sections together with steel. Its telegraph and express services brought about a revolution in communications not only between East and West but also within the West. The railway and its telegraph system furnished the federal government with the means of administering the sprawling young nation: officials could quickly assess conditions in troubled areas and impose the rule of law by dispatching troops.

The CPR, through its Department of Immigration, played a major part in populating the West; its policies helped to determine the extent of immigration and areas of settlement, as well as the ethnic composition of the waves of settlers. By selecting locations for stations, terminals and workshops, CPR management created or doomed urban centres from Lake Superior to the Pacific and decided which would become major cities and international ports. Within those communities to which it gave birth, the CPR's initiatives established the location and character of commercial, industrial and residential districts.

Because of its emphasis on enlightened self-interest, the CPR also played a key role in western agriculture, determining the spread of grain cultivation, the types of seeds used and the design of grain elevators. In addition, the company's Department of Natural Resources undertook North America's largest irrigation project, altering a massive arid region into a productive farming zone.

The CPR's land holdings affected the development and growth of such major western Canadian industries as lumbering, ranching, mining, smelting and petroleum extraction. By building an extensive, modern transportation network, the CPR helped to transform a vast, isolated, sparsely populated and unknown region into millions of acres of farmland sprinkled with bustling towns, as well as providing the means of moving the rich resources of the West to world markets.

While the CPR's influence during the nation's formative years was regarded by some businessmen and farmers as a positive, very productive force in the West, others considered it a chronically monopolistic force that cost them dear and limited their freedom. To the Indians and the Métis, it was one of the major instruments of the white takeover of their homeland. Whatever the feelings and speeches of westerners, there is no question that the Canadian Pacific Railway was the primary force shaping western Canada between 1880 and 1930.

Chapter 1 **The Impossible Railway**

"As early as 1849 . . . " Douglas Owram, *Promise of Eden: The Canadian Expansionist Movement and the Idea of the West, 1856-1900* (Toronto: University of Toronto Press, 1980), 31.

"With the confidence . . . " Terry Coleman, *The Railway Navvies* (London: Penguin Books, 1981), 42.

"That the U.S. are . . . " *Daily Alta. California*, San Francisco, 3 February 1869.

"The rugged land . . . " Don W. Thomson, *Men and Meridians* (Ottawa: Information Canada, 1972), vol. 2, 85.

"Instead of contracted canyon . . . " George Grant, *Ocean to Ocean: Sandford Fleming's Expedition through Canada in 1872* (Reprint, Edmonton: M.G. Hurtig, 1967), 253.

"Immediate, private . . . " *Globe*, Toronto, 18 July 1873.

"It would be at least 100 miles . . . " W. Kaye Lamb, *History of the Canadian Pacific Railway* (New York: Macmillan, 1977), 263-64.

"End of Track was . . . " Peter Turner Bone, *When the Steel Went Through: Reminiscences of a Railway Pioneer* (Toronto: Macmillan of Canada, 1947), 43.

"In fifteen months . . . " *The Saint Paul Pioneer Press*, 15 August 1920.

"We had planned . . . " Bone, *When the Steel Went Through*, 47.

"We had completed . . . " Charles Aeneas Shaw, *Tales of a Pioneer Surveyor* (Toronto: Longmans, 1970), 147-48.

"Onderdonk had brought in . . . " Edgar Wickberg, ed., *From China to Canada: A History of the Chinese Communities in Canada* (Toronto: McClelland and Stewart with the Muilticulturalism Directorate, Department of the Secretary of State, 1982), 20-22.

"Apparently more than 200 Chinese . . . " Ibid., 23.

"At least 600 Chinese . . . " Ibid., 24.

"The bridge to be built . . . " Bone, *When the Steel Went Through*, 95-96.

"In any case, Van Horne . . . " Walter Vaughan, *The Life and Work of Sir William Van Horne* (New York: The Century Co., 1920), 131.

Chapter 2 **Consolidating the Empire**

"The consist . . . " Omer Lavallée, *Van Horne's Road* (Montreal: Railfare, 1974), 252.

"No such vessels . . . " *Owen Sound Advertiser*, 24 April 1884.

"R. B. Angus . . . " George Musk, *Canadian Pacific: The Story of the Famous Shipping Line* (Toronto: Holt, Rinehart, and Winston of Canada, 1981), 15.

Luxury from Sea to Sea

"These cars are of . . . " Canadian Pacific Railway, *The Canadian Pacific: The New Highway to the East* (Montreal, 1888), 46.

Chapter 3 **"The Wondrous West"**

"On my Journey . . . " Account by Apokena, a Blackfoot Indian, of his first trip on the CPR, Rev. John Maclean Papers, United Church Archives, Toronto.

"In the spring of 1886 . . . " Hugh A. Dempsey, *Crowfoot: Chief of the Blackfeet* (Edmonton: M. G. Hurtig, 1972), 147-50; and Lavallée, *Van Horne's Road*, 243.

"Not merely did the company . . . " James Hedges, *Building the Canadian West* (Reprint, New York: Russell and Russell, 1971), 120.

"In 1882, the company issued . . . " Ibid., 322.

"In doing a service . . . " Ibid., 321.

"The wisdom of irrigation . . . " Ibid., 298-99.

"Aware of the decline . . . " Letter from George Stephen to John A. Macdonald, 20 September 1887, Macdonald Papers, vol. 270, Public Archives of Canada.

Lures to a Land of Hope and Beauty

"There is no other portion . . ." William F. Butler, *The Great Lone Land* (London: Sampson Low, 1872), v.

Chapter 4 **A Frontier Tamed**

"Foreseeing the difficulties . . . " Sandford Fleming, *Report on Surveys and Preliminary Operations on the Canadian Pacific Railway Up to January, 1877* (Ottawa, 1877), 78.

"He also warned . . . " Ibid., 79.

"Stations were located . . . " Lamb, *History of the Canadian Pacific Railway*, 86.

"The railway with its unfailing . . . " W. A. Mackintosh, *Prairie Settlement: The Geographical Setting* (Toronto: Macmillan of Canada, 1934), 57.

"Hamilton! Hamilton! . . . " L. A. Hamilton File, J.S. Matthews Collection, Vancouver City Archives.

"Since we can't export . . . " John M. Gibbon, *Steel of Empire: the Romantic History of the Canadian Pacific* (Toronto: McClelland and Stewart, 1935), 304.

Castles in the Wilderness

"There is nothing of . . . " Douglas P. Sladen, *On the Cars and Off: Being the Journal of a Pilgrimage Along the Queen's Highway to the East* (London: Ward, Lock and Bowden, 1895), 306-7.

"A large and handsome . . . " Canadian Pacific Railway, *The Canadian Pacific: The New Highway to the Orient* (Montreal, 1890), 46.

ILLUSTRATION CREDITS

We gratefully acknowledge the courtesy of various institutions and individuals in granting permission to reproduce items from their collections. Illustrations are listed by page number, from top to bottom, left to right. Principal sources are credited under the following abbreviations:

ACR   Archives of the Canadian Rockies
CPCA   Canadian Pacific Corporate Archives
CRM   Canadian Railway Museum
GA   Glenbow Archives
GL   Glenbow Library
IPB   Interior Photo Bank at Kelowna Centennial Museum
NPA   Notman Photographic Archives
PABC   Provincial Archives of British Columbia
PAC   Public Archives of Canada
VCA   Vancouver City Archives
VMM   Vancouver Maritime Museum

Endpapers: Both sides of a two-sided map published by the CPR in 1927. GL 104.2 1927 C213

Half-title page: At the Little Tunnel on the Kettle Valley Railway, 1914. IPB Vernon Board of Museum and Archives

Frontispiece: The CPR main line near Exshaw, North West Territories, 1885. GA NA-4140-13
Title page: Passengers on the pilot beam of a locomotive, Field, B.C. GA NA-4281-1

Illustrations in the margins of the main text are all from the Glenbow Library, with the exception of the one on page 59, which is reproduced courtesy of Parks Canada.

/10-11 CRM 17 /24-25 PAC C-2787, PABC 62506 /26 PAC PA-22618 /27 PAC PA-65409 /28-29 Provincial Archives of Manitoba N14 /30 NPA MP177 /31 GA NA-1315-5, Provincial Archives of Manitoba and GA NA-1315-4 /32 PABC 75081, PABC 19661, NPA MP013/79 /34 GA NA-782-11 /35 GA NA-573-7, CPCA A4421 /36 CPCA A4406, CPCA A4402 /37 GA NA-2856-2 /38-39 GA NA-782-9 /40 GA NA-531-5 /41 GA NA-782-5, CRM 31 /42-43 CRM 34 /44-45 GA NA-4428-3, GA NA-3688-12 /46 GA NA-1494(a) /47 CPCA 1340 /49 GAD Man 60.76.1, PABC pdp4450 /50 PABC pdp4901 /51 PABC pdp3874, PABC pdp4687 /52 GA C81508 /53 GAD IJ 60.71.20 /54 PABC pdp4467 /55 CP Hotels /56-57 GA NA-4140-39 /67 VCA /68-69 CRM, GA NA-4140-56 /70 GA NA-387-21 /71 GA NA-4428-17 /72 GA NA-1459-3 /73 GA NC-2-272, GA NC-2-273 /74 GA NA-990-1 /75 IPB Gill Collection 2647, GA NA-4432-8 /76 GA NA-1248-34, GA NA-1753-22 /77 GA NA-1248-26 /78 CPCA 1, CPCA 33 /79 CPCA 16648, CPCA 12168, CPCA 19197 /80 Provincial Archives of Manitoba N2620, IPB Vernon Board of Museum and Archives /81 IPB Kelowna Branch of Okanagan Historical Society /82 GA NA-387-31 /83 GA NA-1753-23 /84 VMM N1602, VMM /85 Maritime Museum of British Columbia /86-87 GA NA-1794-1 /88 GA NA-1263-36, CPCA A11370, PAC PA-38495 /89 CPCA 7193, GA NA-698-3, GA NA-3740-29 /90-91 GA NC-53-438, GA NA-1753-4, PAC PA-42814 /92 GL 385.09 C22cm (1888), GA NA-1083-2 /93 PAC PA-11848 /94 NPA 1505 /95 CPCA 12968 /96-97 CPCA A11367 /98 CPCA 10439, PAC PA-11828, CPCA 10440 /99 CPCA 63 /100 NPA 2520, CPCA A1981 /101 CPCA 15170 /102-103 GA NA-403-1 /112-113 PAC C-11336, CPCA Omer Lavallée Collection and GA NA-448-3 /114 CRM 4 /115 CRM 10, GA NA-3700-3 /116 GA NA-1043-1 /117 CPCA 16354, CPCA 12974, GA NA-3341-3 /118 PAC C-63257, PAC C-9671 /119 GA NA-2878-4 /120-121 GA NA-984-2 /122 Centre for Mennonite Brethren Studies in Canada, GA NA-2829-18 /123 GA NA-3420-1 /124 GA NA-3641-1 /125 GA NA-2179-39 /126-127 GA ND-8-202, GA ND-8-222 /129 GA NA-1459-52 /130 GL Pam 799 C2125f (1896), GL Pam 971.1 C2122sn (1894), GL Pam 799.2 C212f (1893) /131 GL Pam 971.18 R683cp (1909) /132 GL Pam 631.7 C2123i /133 GL Pam 330.9712 C2125b /134 PAC RG76/vol. 41B/f608414 /135 Dr. W. B. Chung /136-137 CRM 19 /150 PAC PA-118764 /151 GA NA-624-4, CPCA 19143, GA NA-118-24 /152 GA NA-3740-4 /153 GA NA-3173-1, GA NA-1044-1 /154 VCA 87 /155 VCA 84 /156 VCA Can P 67/N46 /157 VCA Can P 34/N208, VMM /158-159 IPB, B.C. Ministry of Forests 13939 /160-161 CPCA 1262, GA NB-16-260 /162 CPCA 1656, GA NA-573-9 /163 CPCA 1619 /164 GA NA-1753-24 /165 IPB Vernon Board of Museum and Archives 1820 /166-167 IPB Kelowna Museum /168 GA NA-387-28, GA /169 GA NA-2399-26 /170-171 GA NA-2119-4, GA NA-1072-6 /172 GA /173 GA NA-1798-1, ACR NA-80-981 /174 GA NA-1608-5, GA NA-1798-6, GA /175 ACR NG-4-585, ACR NG-4-583 /176 GA NA-2977-19, GA NA-819-1 /177 GA NA-1263-3 /178-179 GA NA-937-9, ACR NA-71-4864, GA NA-937-9 /180 GA NA-2977-3 /181 GA NA-637-15 /182 GA NA-2126-19 /183 GA NA-3707-34, Banff Springs Hotel, GA NA-714-109 /184-185 GL

Bibliography

Artibise, Alan F. J., ed. *Winnipeg, An Illustrated History*. Toronto: James Lorimer & Co. and National Museum of Man, National Museums of Canada, 1977.

Berton, Pierre. *The Last Spike*. Toronto: McClelland & Stewart, 1971.

Berton, Pierre. *The National Dream*. Toronto: McClelland & Stewart, 1970.

Bone, P. Turner. *When the Steel Went Through: Reminiscences of a Railroad Pioneer*. Toronto: Macmillan, 1947.

Dempsey, Hugh A. *Crowfoot: Chief of the Blackfeet*. Edmonton: M. G. Hurtig, 1976.

Foran, Max. *Calgary, An Illustrated History*. Toronto: James Lorimer & Co. and National Museum of Man, National Museums of Canada, 1978.

Gibbon, John M. *Steel of Empire: the Romantic History of the Canadian Pacific*. Toronto: McClelland and Stewart, 1935.

Gilbert, Heather. *The Life of Lord Mount Stephen*, Vol. 1, *Awakening Continent*. Aberdeen: Aberdeen University Press, 1965.

Gilbert, Heather. *The Life of Lord Mount Stephen*, Vol. 2, *The End of the Road*. Aberdeen: Aberdeen University Press, 1977.

Hacking, Norman R., and W. Kaye Lamb. *The Princess Story, A Century and a Half of West Coast Shipping*. Vancouver: Mitchell Press Ltd., 1974.

Hedges, James. *Building the Canadian West, The Land and Colonization Policies of the Canadian Pacific Railway*. New York: Russell and Russell, 1971.

Lamb, W. Kaye. *History of the Canadian Pacific Railway*. New York: Macmillan, 1977.

Lavallée, Omer. *Van Horne's Road*. Montreal: Railfare, 1974.

Luxton, Eleanor G. *Banff, Canada's First National Park, A History and Memory of Rocky Mountain Park*. Banff: Summerthought, 1975.

Musk, George. *Canadian Pacific: The Story of the Famous Shipping Line*. Toronto: Holt, Rinehart, and Winston of Canada, 1981.

McBeth, R. G. *The Romance of the Canadian Pacific Railway*. Toronto: The Ryerson Press, 1924.

Reid, Dennis. *Our Own Country Canada, Being an Account of the National Aspirations of the Principal Landscape Artists in Montreal and Toronto, 1860-1900*. Ottawa: National Gallery of Canada, National Museums of Canada, 1979.

Roy, Patricia. *Vancouver, An Illustrated History*. Toronto: James Lorimer & Co. and National Museum of Man, National Museums of Canada, 1980.

Shaw, Charles Aeneas. *Tales of a Pioneer Surveyor*. Toronto: Longman's, 1970.

Turner, Robert D. *The Pacific Princesses*. Victoria: Sono Nis Press, 1977.

Turner, Robert D. *The Pacific Princesses*. Victoria: Sono Nis Press, 1981.

Thomson, Don W. *Men and Meridians*. Ottawa: Information Canada, 1972.

Vaughan, Walter. *The Life and Work of Sir William Van Horne*, New York: The Century Co., 1920.

Whyte, Jon, and Carole Harmon. *Lake Louise, A Diamond in the Wilderness*. Banff: Altitude Publishing, 1982.

Wickberg, Edgar, ed. *From China to Canada: A History of the Chinese Communities in Canada*. Toronto: McClelland and Stewart in association with the Multiculturalism Directorate, Department of the Secretary of State, 1982.

Willson, Beckles. *The Life of Lord Strathcona and Mount Royal*, Vol. 1. Boston: Houghton Mifflin, 1915.

References to illustrations are in italic type.